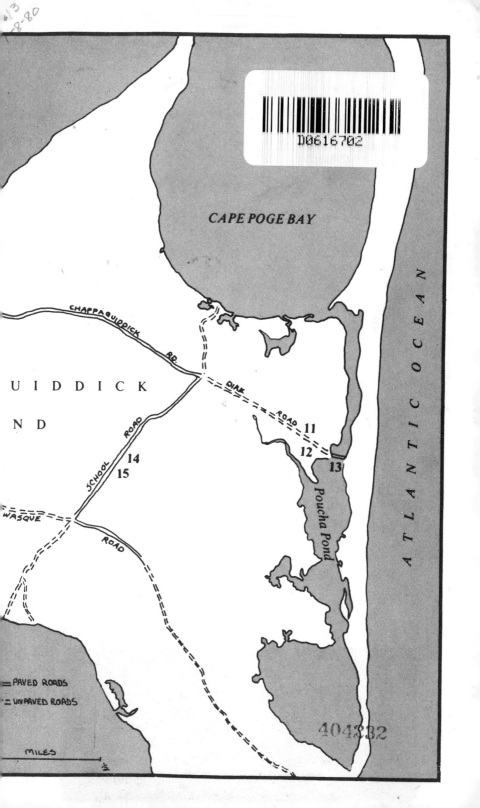

CAPE POGE BAY

ATLANTIC OCEAN

CHAPPAQUIDDICK RD.

UIDDICK
ND

DIKE ROAD

11

12

13

SCHOOL ROAD

14
15

WASQUE

ROAD

Poucha Pond

PAVED ROADS
UNPAVED ROADS

MILES
½

DEATH AT CHAPPAQUIDDICK

by

Richard L. Tedrow

and

Thomas L. Tedrow

Caroline House Publishers, Inc.
Ottawa, Illinois & Thornwood, New York

Death at Chappaquiddick

Caroline House Publishers, Inc.

Library of Congress Catalogue Number: 76-3349.

Manufactured in the United States of America.
ISBN: 0-916054-28-4

Third Printing, January 1979

As we send this manuscript to the publisher in early January, 1976, events are running true to form. It has been reported in the Press that all police records and papers of this internationally famous case have disappeared from the official files in Edgartown, Massachusetts. A still later report says they were located in Maine in the possession of an ex-Police Chief who said he needed them to answer questions.

— R. L. T. & T. L. T.

Table of Contents

The Beginning of the End

DURING THE EVENING of July 18, 1969, Senator Edward Kennedy attended a private party on Chappaquiddick Island. He left the party with Mary Jo Kopechne some time between 11:15 p.m. and 12:45 a.m. on July 19, 1969. They drove toward an isolated beach, but never made it because Senator Kennedy's car went off the Dyke Bridge[1] into Poucha Pond. He emerged alive and took almost ten hours to report the accident. Mary Jo did not escape from his submerged car and died sometime during the night. Her death has been the only certainty in the tragedy. Everything else has been shrouded in contradiction, controversy and denials.

We believe this book is the most complete account of Chappaquiddick. Through research, investigation and study we have tried to answer all the major questions this tragedy has raised. Many will find the answers unpleasant and the issues shocking, but truth is always hard to accept if it is unwanted.

Because Senator Kennedy will probably run for the Presidency of the United States one day, it is essential that all questions about Chappaquiddick be answered. The Presidency is the hardest job in the nation; it takes a man in complete control of his actions, his mental faculties and his moral direction. Senator Kennedy deserves to be judged on his own personal abilities and not on those of his brothers or on his family name.

[1] It may be noted that certain proper names are spelled in more than one way in this work. The official court record shows these various spellings and they are used here to lend historical authenticity.

2 / Beginning

We believe that Chappaquiddick is both the beginning and the end for Senator Kennedy. It will be the central issue in any national campaign in which he is involved. In this case, the facts draw their own conclusion. Chappaquiddick is the Senator's own doing, and may be the undoing of his presidential ambitions. It is a very serious issue that shows how a potential President of the United States reacted during his time of crisis. For this reason, Chappaquiddick cannot be ignored.

Part One

Aftermath

THE PRIVATE PARTY

SENATOR KENNEDY WAS at Chappaquiddick on July 18 and 19, 1969, for two reasons. The first was his family tradition of participating in the annual Edgartown Sailing Regatta. The second and more important reason was the carefully planned private party in the Lawrence cottage on isolated Chappaquiddick Island.[1]

To ensure privacy the party arrangements were made in advance by different Kennedy loyalists without mentioning the Senator's name. The fame of the Kennedys necessitates this type of planning. Jack Crimmins, a Kennedy chauffeur, reserved rooms for the party guests at the Dunes Hotel. The guests were six young, single girls who had worked for Robert Kennedy and had remained close to the Kennedy causes after his assassination. Mary Jo Kopechne was one of these girls.

The party cottage was rented by the Senator's cousin, Joe Gargan, who told the rental agent that it was for himself, his wife and another couple. Between the time of the rental and the party, the plans apparently changed somewhat.

Senator Kennedy had reservations at the Shiretown Inn, where he stayed whenever he visited Edgartown. Gargan made these reservations for the Senator. To Russ Peachy and Bill Parker, co-owners of the Shiretown Inn, Gargan meant Kennedy. When he called it was to signal another Kennedy booking and to signal them to prepare the welcome.

Senator Kennedy left Washington, D.C. at 10:40 a.m. on Friday, July 18. He arrived at Martha's Vineyard at 1:30 p.m. As always, Jack Crimmins chauffeured him from the small airport to the Lawrence cottage on Chappaquiddick Island,

---

[1] Judge Boyle found in his inquest report: "Kennedy was the host and mainly responsible for the assembly of the group at Edgartown."

which is accessible only by a small, two-car ferry. The Senator wanted to change into his bathing suit and join the girls for a quick swim before the regatta.

To get to the isolated beach, the Senator followed the same route that would change history later that night. Crimmins drove down the paved School Road, making a sharp right onto the rough and unpaved Dike Road. After a bumpy drive, they took Dike Bridge across Poucha Pond to the beach.

After an hour or so on the beach with Mary Jo Kopechne and her five friends, Senator Kennedy went back across Dike Bridge to change clothes and participate in the regatta from 2:30 until 6:00 p.m. The six girls followed the Senator's regatta in a chartered boat and shouted him encouragement along the way. Though Senator Kennedy did not win, everyone had a great time.

When the race was over, Senator Kennedy checked into his rooms at the Shiretown Inn to change clothes. Ross Richards, Stanley Moore and several crew members dropped by to discuss the race over beer and drinks in his room. The small get-together occupied the Senator's time from 6:30 until around 7:00 p.m.

Crimmins picked Senator Kennedy up and delivered him to the Lawrence cottage by 7:30, so he could bathe and freshen up for the party. By 8:30, everyone had arrived for the cookout, drinking and good times. We know now[1] that those present were:

NAME	AGE	MARITAL STATUS
Senator Kennedy	37	married
Paul Markham	39	married
Ray LaRosa	41	married
Charlie Tretter	30	married
Joe Gargan	39	married
Jack Crimmins	63	single

[1] "For days Kennedy sources refused to divulge the names of those who attended. . . . After several days, it was learned that six men and six women attended." *Human Events,* August 2, 1969.

Rosemary Keough	23	single
Suzie Tannenbaum	24	single
Esther Newberg	26	single
Nance Lyons	26	single
Maryellen Lyons	27	single
Mary Jo Kopechne	28	single

Details of the party are contradictory, depending on when one talked with the girls. Immediately after the accident, they told reporters it was the kind of party where no one watched the clock or who was where, or with whom. At the inquest six months later, it became a dull, clockwatching affair. Most reports indicate that it was not a dull party, but was rather loud and long. Residents of Chappaquiddick said the party was "one of those loud, noisy brawls."[1]

It does not seem to be a coincidence that the five older, married men and the chauffeur got together with the six younger, single girls at the isolated cottage. All had opportunity to leave if the arrangements were unsatisfactory. Many reports conclude that all twelve knew what was planned and that they were prepared to enjoy an all-night island party. To support this, they show that there was no effort by the group to catch the last ferry back to their motel rooms in Edgartown.

The party was well stocked with steaks and liquor. By 10:00 p.m., the Silvas, who lived 150 yards away, could hear quite a blast in progress. Dodie Silva remarked to her family: "Boy, they must be having a heck of a time. . . . I hope they don't wreck the place." By 1:30 a.m., John Silva was ready to call the police in to halt the "disturbance". "There was yelling, music and general sounds of hell-raising."[2]

After all, it was an island summer night, away from the press and pains of political life in Washington. It was a time to celebrate. American Apollo astronauts were speeding towards man's first moon walk, and most of the party members had watched Senator Kennedy maintain the family tradition of not winning the regatta.

To celebrate, Crimmins had bought at least three half-gallons of vodka, four fifths of scotch, two half-gallons of

[1] *Human Events*, August 2, 1969.
[2] *Ibid.*

rum[1], and three cases of beer. This figures out to a quart of liquor plus a six-pack of beer for each of the twelve party members.

Whenever the party ended on Saturday, a great deal of liquor had been consumed, even though no one there admitted to drinking much of it. Two half-gallons of rum were gone, though only Kennedy (two doubles[2]) and Crimmins (three drinks) said they drank rum. A fifth of scotch disappeared although LaRosa had only one drink and Rosemary Keough had but two drinks. A half-gallon of vodka evaporated although Newberg had only two, Nancy Lyons two, Markham one, and Tannenbaum two drinks. Even more liquor could have mysteriously drained away, because we have only Crimmins' word on what he bought. At the island dump near the party cottage, Tony Bettencourt, who was in charge of the rubbish area, found several gin bottles on Saturday among what appeared to be the party remains.

How much liquor was consumed at the party has been a questionable point. Since there were no breath tests, blood tests or immediate questioning of the living party members by Massachusetts authorities, the credibility of the witnesses is at stake. All of the party members described Mary Jo by reputation and action at the party as a light drinker.

However, the Massachusetts State Police lend unexpected help in this matter. It is an analysis of Mary Jo's blood before her body was taken off the island and buried. The analysis showed the alcoholic content at nine-tenths of one percent, which is equivalent to almost five ounces of 80 to 90 proof liquor consumed within an hour by a person of 110 pounds. If the person had been drinking more than an hour, the amount of consumed liquor increases. The party started at 8:30 p.m. and was still going strong at 1:30 a.m. Kennedy poured Mary Jo's first drink around 8:35 p.m.

Compared to what the others say they drank that night, Mary Jo's blood analysis shows her to be the heaviest drinker

---

[1] Some reports have said the amount of rum was in quarts or fifths. From evidence shown, we believe it was half-gallons.

[2] At the inquest, Senator Kennedy was asked, "What amount of rum did you put in (your drink)?" He answered, " . . . I suppose two ounces."

of the party. This contradicts her reputation as a social drinker.

The question of drinking plays an important part in this scenario. By clean-up time Saturday morning, about 14-16 ounces of liquor per person was gone, although by their sworn testimony the partygoers had only two drinks each. This makes Mary Jo a real lush — but all of the others agreed she drank the least.

This leaves us with the known scientific fact that alcohol evaporates when opened and exposed to the air, but disappears even more quickly when exposed to people. Where did all the whiskey go, when asked after a party, is one of the questions that modern science still cannot answer. (As one reporter said, we have here the greatest disappearance of booze since Prohibition.)

You have to decide whether those party people told the truth about how much they individually and collectively drank. Questions of by whom and how much liquor was consumed are important in any automobile accident case. They are of particular importance at Chappaquiddick where the death of Mary Jo Kopechne is involved.

There has been wide speculation that Senator Kennedy was not just intoxicated but loaded when he drove off Dike Bridge that night. His past reputation in the whiskey line has never been too good, although there have been worse in both the House and the Senate. The Congress has always had exponents of the cup that cheers from Daniel Webster of Massachusetts and his often Bacchus-inspired oratory, through Cactus Jack Garner striking blows for liberty, right up to the recent incident of Wild Bill Mills chasing a filly into the Washington Tidal Basin waterhole.

Some of the Chappaquiddick gossip has said that the nine-hour delay in reporting the accident was needed to sober up the Senator. Others say it was needed to sober up everyone at the party. Regardless of how much of such gossip is true, there is no question that whiskey consumption is important and involved in this case.

Joseph Kennedy, Senior, made millions out of liquor, but never drank himself. He was actually hostile towards drinking and offered his sons $1,000 apiece if they would refrain from drinking until they were 21. Whether anyone collected is not immediately known, but neither John nor Bobby had any reputation for trouble in this area. Their drinking seems to have been generally of the social type.

Brother Ted is of a different temperament, and has had problems in the past. Different authors recount various episodes on this, although before Chappaquiddick the daily press either ignored or buried such items. Senator Kennedy's reputation and the resulting incidents have not been any secret from the locals of Hyannis Port and Edgartown, and certainly not from the Senator's aides and intimates.

One episode not reported in the press took place on a small commercial airplane with passengers aboard.[1] Senator Kennedy was returning from Alaska in the Spring of '68 after a subcommittee investigation of Indian education. For whatever reason, the Senator really tied one on. He never stopped drinking from Fairbanks, Alaska, to Washington, D.C. Senator Kennedy was so loud and offensive, running up and down the aisle cheering "Eskimo Power," that his aides could not handle him. One Kennedy staffer has been quoted as saying they lost 60 potential national election votes every time that sort of thing happened.[2]

In fairness to the press, it generally gives these 'breaks' of silence to public officials for personal failings involving women and whiskey. This is done until the conduct becomes such that it cannot be ignored. A case in point is the reporting in late 1974 of an interview with the Chairman of the House Ways and Means Committee after his "stage debut" in a Boston burlesque house when he should have been back in Congress tending to the affairs of the nation. A similar incident occurred before his 1974 re-election, and the press, by covering over his past losing fights with the bottle, did the people of Arkansas and the nation a disservice. No one is naive enough to think this situation arose overnight. It had been common knowledge in official circles and to the press all

[1] Burton Hersh, *The Education of Edward Kennedy*, pp. 379, 380, and Jack Olsen, *The Bridge at Chappaquiddick*, p. 60.

[2] Olsen, *Ibid.*

along. Yet, in this country "for the people," we are the last to find out and are always hurt more by the delay.[1]

Certain members of Congress regularly spend time "drying out" in the Naval Hospital at Bethesda, Maryland. The office staff hands out a little fiction about a medical check-up or even a needed rest from "overwork". When the press is understanding, then the voters, like the complacent spouse, are the last ones to learn the facts of life. This analogy may be closer to Chappaquiddick and the cast involved than you think. All three of the Kennedy brothers reaped great benefits from the silent treatment by the press.

The press did report the tidbits from Washington weekends at Hickory Hill when Teddy was pushing a few New Frontiersmen into the swimming pool. These were fed to the public as the humorous hijinks of the great.

The public generally has not been concerned with the drinking angle in Ted Kennedy's life—mainly because it had no knowledge of it. However, there has been concern on the part of insiders—his friends, aides and advisors—who see the Senator, the surviving Kennedy brother, as their last hope for restoration of Kennedy power in the White House.

Thus, it is very important that all aspects of alcohol at Chappaquiddick be considered. If material facts have been withheld from the case or destroyed, then we are obliged to use any available information—including past reputation—to come up with the truth. A lot of alcohol disappeared from that party. What part it played in the Senator's conduct, driving, and delay in reporting the accident may be very important.

---

[1] Nor did the least hint appear in the press about the romance with Marilyn Monroe of John and Bobby, in that order, although Miss Monroe was telling intimates she was going to be Robert Kennedy's First Lady.

THE MIDNIGHT RIDE

THE PARTY was a welcome relief for everyone. They all left the problems and worries of Washington, their jobs and their families behind for a few short hours. The dancing, drinking and singing mixed well with the isolated island atmosphere. Many people have hinted that the party was planned so that they could pair off and make a night of it. Senator Kennedy later denied such speculation:

> I know of nothing in Mary Jo's conduct on that or any other occasion — the same is true of the other girls at the party — that would lend any substance to such ugly speculation about their character.[1]

In the 1974 series of interviews with the *Boston Globe,* in the aftermath of Watergate, the Senator flatly denied that the cookout party was a "married man's night out." Still, the situation and setting of the party, by its very nature, breeds doubts. Jack Anderson says, "Before the accident, the revelers began drifting off in twos and threes for midnight drives and strolls."[2]

Senator Kennedy claims that he decided to leave the party at about 11:15 so that he could catch the last ferry back to Edgartown. He wanted to get a good night's sleep before Saturday's race. Mary Jo wanted to go along because she was not feeling well.

At the inquest, Senator Kennedy said:

> At 11:15 I was talking with Miss Kopechne, perhaps for some minutes before that period of time. I noticed the time, desired

---

[1] Nationwide television speech, Edward Kennedy, July 25, 1969.
[2] Jack Anderson, "Washington Merry-Go-Round," September 26, 1969.

to leave and return to the Shiretown Inn and indicated to her that I was leaving and returning to town. She indicated to me that she was desirous of leaving, if I would be kind enough to drop her back at her hotel. I said, well, I'm leaving immediately; spoke with Mr. Crimmins, requested the keys for the car and left at that time.

Q. Does Mr. Crimmins usually drive your car or drive you?

A. On practically every occasion.

Q. On practically every occasion?

A. Yes.

Q. Was there anything in particular that changed those circumstances at this particular time?

A. Only to the extent that Mr. Crimmins, as well as some of the other fellows that were attending the cookout, were concluding their meal, enjoying the fellowship, and it didn't appear to me to be necessary to require him to bring me back to Edgartown.[1]

The stories told by Senator Kennedy, the partygoers and island neighbors do not match up. The party can not be both a dull affair and a wild blast at the same time. Senator Kennedy has staked out the middle ground between the two, but still leaves the truth in limbo.

The Senator and Mary Jo left the party and got into his black Oldsmobile 88. In sworn testimony, Kennedy said their destination was to catch the last ferry back to Edgartown. However, the Senator says, he was unfamiliar with the road and made a wrong turn towards the beach, the bridge and the fatal accident.

In his first statement to the police, Senator Kennedy said:

On July 18, 1969, at approximately 11:15 p.m. on Chappaquiddick Island, Martha's Vineyard, I was driving my car on Main Street on my way to get the ferry back to Edgartown. I

[1] See complete text of inquest in this book, pages 99-147.

was unfamiliar with the road and turned right onto Dike Road, instead of bearing hard left on Main Street.

The Senator's claim that he and Mary Jo left the party at about 11:15 to catch the ferry is widely doubted, because of inconsistencies and eye-witness reports. Questions of Senator Kennedy's and Mary Jo's departure time and destination have been the subjects of a great deal of critical hashing and re-hashing in the press. Minutes have been counted, added, subtracted and invented. Few people have any real illusions about the actual time of the arrival at Dike Road and the destination. There should be none. We will show that if the Senator's accident timetable is *moved up just one hour*, everything falls right into place.

At the inquest, the testimony of Deputy Sheriff Look stands out above all else in the 763-page transcript. Look's testimony is a breath of fresh air because it can be viewed without any political implications or motivations. *Before the Kennedy car had been pulled from the water the next morning,* Deputy Look had reported what he had seen. Look testified that at about 12:45 a.m. on July 19, he saw a "dark colored" car with two people in the front seat, "and also either another person or an object of clothing, a handbag or something, sitting on the back." Look said:

> . . .the car passed directly in front of me about 35 feet away from my car, my headlights were on this car, and right across and then stopped. I continued around the corner and stopped and I noticed the car lights were backing up, and I said to myself, Well, they probably want some information; so I stopped my car and got out and started to walk back to them on Cemetery Road. I got about 25 or 30 feet when the car was backing up and backed toward the ferry landing on the macadamized road, and then it drove down the Dyke Road.

Look testified that the dark car had a Massachusetts license number that "began with an L and had a 7 at the beginning and one at the end." The Kennedy license number was L78-207.

The next morning when they were pulling Kennedy's car from Poucha Pond, Look testified:

> As soon as they started to pull it out and it became visible, I walked over and told Officer Brougier, gee, that is the same car I saw last night. . . I didn't examine it that closely. I just looked quickly and decided in my own mind that was the same one I had seen and I walked over and mentioned it to Officer Brougier.

Compare Look's sworn testimony to Kennedy's sworn testimony and you decide who is telling the truth:

Q. And when you left the house at Chappaquiddick at 11:15, you were driving?

A. That is correct.

Q. And where was Miss Kopechne seated?

A. In the front seat.

Q. Was there any other person—was there any other person in that car at that time?

A. No.

Q. Was there any other item, thing or object in the car at that time of any size?

A. Well, not to my knowledge at that particular time. I have read subsequently in newspapers that there was another person in that car, but that is only what I have read about, and to my knowledge at that time there wasn't any other object that I was aware of.

Q. Well, Senator, was there any other person in the car?

A. No, there was not.

Q. And on leaving the cottage, Senator—Mr. Kennedy, where did you go?

A. Well, I traveled down, I believe it is Main Street, took a right on Dyke Road and drove off the bridge at Dyke Bridge.

Q. Did you at any time drive into Cemetery Road?

A. At no time did I drive into Cemetery Road.

Q. Did you back that car up at any time?

A. At no time did I back that car up.

Q. Did you see anyone on the road between the cottage and the bridge that night?

A. I saw no one on the road between the cottage and the bridge.

Q. Did you stop the car at any time?

A. I did not stop the car at any time.

Q. Did you pass any other vehicle at that time?

A. I passed no other vehicle at that time. I passed no other vehicle and I saw no other person and I did not stop the car at any time between the time I left the cottage and went off the bridge.

Q. Now, would you describe your automobile to the court?

A. Well, it is a four-door black sedan, Oldsmobile.

Q. Do you recall the registration plate?

A. I do not recall the registration plate.

In this age of computers, it should have been fairly easy to settle the Look-Kennedy testimony contradictions. Massachusetts officials could have eliminated all cars which did not have the following characteristics: Massachusetts plates, L7-7 plate numbers; dark, four-door sedan; presence on Chappaquiddick Island at 12:45 a.m. on July 19 on the road leading to Dyke Bridge, having two people in the front seat. Most people feel it would have eliminated all but one car — Senator Kennedy's car. Since the police investigation revealed that the ferry operator took no car that matched Look's description to Chappaquiddick after 12:30 a.m., and took none back before or during the accident,[1] then the mystery double car should still be hiding somewhere on the small Chappaquiddick Island.

Judge Boyle addressed himself to the possibility of eliminating all but the guilty car in his inquest findings. It was decided against, because "... there would be no assurance that the end result would be helpful and, in any event, the elimination of all other cars within the registration group (although it would seriously affect the credibility of some of the witnesses) would not alter the findings of this report." Many people believe that an answer would have been "helpful," that it "would seriously affect the credibility of some of the witnesses," and that such an answer would definitely alter the entire case and testimony of the Kennedy group.

If Senator Kennedy and Mary Jo were returning to their motel rooms, why didn't Mary Jo tell her friends? Why didn't she take her purse or ask Esther Newberg for the room key? If the party was not an all-night affair, why would Kennedy and Mary Jo take the large Oldsmobile, leaving ten people to ride back in the small, rented Valiant? Was it because, as Jack Anderson said, they were both going down a familiar road and "were heading for a look at or a dip in the ocean."[2]

Though Kennedy said he told no one other than Crimmins about their departure so as not to break up the party prematurely, were the others then planning to spend the night on the island? Since the ferry normally closed at midnight, and the Senator supposedly left to catch it, is he acknowledging that the others had no intention of leaving? With no other public way of getting back to Edgartown, the Senator leaves us with not much choice.

[1] Jared Grant, who operates the ferry that Senator Kennedy claims he was trying to catch, was looking for the Senator to return. Though he normally closed at midnight, he spent the evening of the 18th waiting for Kennedy, remaining open until 12:45, and not leaving the ferry until 1:20 a.m.

[2] Jack Anderson, "Washington Merry-Go-Round," September 26, 1969.

Jack Anderson and many others conclude that "Mary Jo did not take her purse along on the midnight drive because, contrary to the Senator's statement, she intended to return to the cottage. To prevent Kennedy from being caught in a lie, someone apparently removed the purse from the cottage the next morning."[1]

The purse was later found and returned to Mary Jo's parents many months later. If there was nothing to hide, then why was the purse presumably hidden at some time between the accident and when the officials began their investigation the next morning?

Senator Kennedy is sure that they left the party at 11:15. Were others at the party equally certain? It is interesting to read what Esther Newberg told reporters on July 23rd, five days after the accident. Several reporters were present, working on a major story with very little information. They questioned Miss Newberg on the time that the Senator and Mary Jo left the party.

Warren Weaver, Jr., a reporter for *The New York Times*, wrote: "Miss Newberg described it as an informal group, with no one keeping particular track of who was there or who wasn't there at any given time. Thus, she said, no one specifically missed either the Senator or Miss Kopechne or noticed what time they had left."

Reporters for the *Chicago Tribune* wrote: "Miss Newberg said she was very vague about time during the evening partly because her watch was a psychedelic one and 'you couldn't read it' and because no one was sitting around watching the clock. . . . 'At no time were we aware of time,' she explained."

The *Worcester Evening Gazette* reporter wrote: "Miss Newberg said she did not notice when Senator Kennedy and Miss Kopechne left the party. . . . She said she did not know the time accurately because her Mickey Mouse watch — which had been a topic of joking conversation — was not working properly."

Six months later at the inquest, *under oath*, Miss Newberg changed her story. Instead of getting fuzzy on the details after many months, she became exact. She told the Assistant Dis-

[1] Jack Anderson, "Washington Merry-Go-Round," September 26, 1969.

trict Attorney she was certain they left at about 11:30 because, "I have a rather large watch that I wear all the time and I looked at it."

Her description of the party also changed at the inquest. Where she had been drinking it up and having a good time, she became a clock watcher. Though she couldn't remember seeing the Senator and Mary Jo leave five days after the accident, six months later she testified under oath, "I saw them walk out of the cottage . . . I saw him walk out. . . . Miss Kopechne was directly behind him."

The other girls had also contradicted the Senator after the accident, but at the inquest they all duly fell into line. Though people were going in and out of the cottage all during the party, each girl — whether she really was even in the cottage at the time or not — protected the Senator by corroborating his testimony.

Deputy Sheriff Look spotted the Senator's car turning towards Dyke Bridge at 12:45, an hour and a half after the Senator's claim of leaving at 11:15. How could the Senator have been seen leaving the cottage at 11:15, and seen by Sheriff Look turning down Dyke Road at 12:45? Many will state flatly that Senator Kennedy and the other party members committed perjury many times throughout the legal proceedings involving this accident.

Look's testimony also contradicts that of the girls. After spotting the Senator's car at 12:45, he said, he drove toward his home and came across a man and two young women doing a "hootchy-kootchy" in the road. Since it was the regatta week-end and many people got lost, he stopped to offer them a ride to where they were staying. To his surprise, he was crudely rebuked by the women who appeared to him to be "loaded." The man, noticing his police insignia, quickly said, "No, thank you sir, we're only going right over here", and pointed to the Lawrence cottage. LaRosa and Nancy and Maryellen Lyons testified that while out for a late night stroll, someone offered them a ride. How could they have seen Kennedy leave the party, if they were out for a walk?

Dr. Donald R. Mills, the medical examiner, was another who told one story after the accident and then changed his story at the inquest, helping the Senator. *Time* quotes Dr. Mills as saying, shortly after the discovery of the submerged car, that "Mary Jo could have died anywhere from five to eight hours — and at the very outside, nine hours. . . ." before he examined her body at 9:30 a.m. Saturday morning. That would put her death anywhere between 12:30 a.m. and 4:30 a.m. — a fact that corroborates Look's eye-witness account and gives support to the national nightmare that Mary Jo was trapped alive in the car.

Then, Mills was as sure of this as he was of the cause of death. By the time of the inquest, he had changed his story — no longer discrediting the Senator — and said that Mary Jo had been found dead "six or more hours" with no outside time limits to entrap the Senator.

The Senator has to insist on leaving at 11:15, because the ferry normally closed at midnight. He could not have known that Jared Grant would hold the ferry for him till 1:20. If the Senator left after midnight, then there is no ferry to catch. If there is no ferry to catch, then there is no use trying to claim that turning down Dyke Road to the Beach was a mistake. If there was no turning down Dyke Road by mistake, then the eyes of the nation widen at the thought of the married Senator and a single girl on the way to a deserted beach after midnight.

No one—not Judge Boyle, reporters who have driven the same route, or the various authors who have written books on the accident — believe that the Senator turned down Dyke Road by mistake. Even if he wasn't familiar with the area, the facts are against him.

First, let's review Senator Kennedy's testimony about turning down the wrong road by mistake, and then refute it:

Q. Do you recall how fast you were driving when you made the right on Dyke Road?

A. No, I would say approximately seven or eight miles an hour.

Q. Well, were you aware at the time that you were driving on a dirt road when you hit, when you turned onto Dyke Road?

A. Well, sometime during the drive down Dyke Road I was aware that I was on the unpaved road, yes.

Q. At what point, Mr. Kennedy, did you realize that you were driving on a dirt road?

A. Just sometime when I was — I don't remember any specific time when I knew I was driving on an unpaved road. I was generally aware sometime during the going down that road that it was unpaved. . . .

Q. When you left the house at 11:15 what was your destination?

A. The Katama Shores, the ferry slip, the Katama Shores, Shiretown.

Q. Now, had you been over that road from the ferry slip to the cottage more than once that day?

A. Yes, I had.

Q. Did you recall at the time that you noticed you were driving on a dirt road, that the road from the ferry slip to the house had been paved?

A. Yes.

THE COURT — I'm going to ask one question. At any time after you got on the unpaved road, the so-called Dyke Road, did you have a realization that you were on the wrong road?

A. No.

Personal observation is enough to refute this absurd testimony. First of all, Main Street is the *only* paved road on the island; Dyke Road has a rough, washboard, dirt surface that shakes any car. The change is noticed immediately. Before you can get on Dyke Road, you have to ignore the way Main Street purposely banks toward the ferry to help you stay on the road. There is also a prominent left-turn sign — a reflecting glass arrow, clearly visible. If you miss the sign, you still have to search to find Dyke Road. It is past the ferry curve and is hidden by bushes.

Once you find Dyke Road, you have to slow down to at least 10 miles per hour to make the abrupt, 90-degree right turn — the turn that Kennedy claims to have made "by mistake."[1] Once you make the difficult maneuver onto Dyke Road and notice the change, there are several driveways that you can turn around in if you want to go back to the ferry — though Kennedy said he couldn't find a place to turn around. It is fair to say that any driver who is not under some kind of influence would immediately notice the change from asphalt to bumpy dirt. The Senator's claim to have turned by mistake sheds doubt on his entire story.

Though Senator Kennedy testified that he was unfamiliar with Chappaquiddick Island, this has been disputed. *Time,* Jack Anderson, *The New York Times* and others have all said that Senator Kennedy and the late John F. Kennedy had for years frequently come to Chappaquiddick. It is their contention that, having been on the island many times before, Senator Kennedy was familiar with it.[2]

---

[1] *Human Events,* August 2, 1969.

[2] In his inquest findings, Judge Boyle stated: "I believe it probable that Kennedy knew of the hazard that lay ahead of him on Dyke Road. . . . Also, if Kennedy knew of this hazard, his operation of the vehicle constituted criminal conduct."

THE LOST HOUR

IF SENATOR KENNEDY and Mary Jo did leave the party at 11:15, then there is a lost hour and a half to account for. They were seen at about 12:45 by Deputy Look at the intersection of School Road and Cemetery Road.

Senator Kennedy and Mary Jo sped off down Dyke Road after spotting Look's car. Look knew that the driver of the black car had clearly seen him and was racing away to avoid contact with the law. As history knows, Senator Kennedy drove off the bridge in the splash heard round the world — give or take nine or ten hours. Evidence points to the conclusion that they were deliberately heading for the beach. Senator Kennedy drove off the bridge through a mixture of carelessness, inattention, nervousness over the police and/or lack of sobriety.

So, between 11:15 when witnesses have sworn they left, and 12:45 when Deputy Look spotted them, there is an hour and a half to fill in. There has been, and probably will continue to be, a lot of rumors and smirking about sex at Chappaquiddick — this is an important aspect to consider in filling in the lost hour. The Senator has found it advisable on several occasions to emphatically deny there was ever any hanky-panky going on, but cynics take a line from Shakespeare and say, "Methinks he doth protest too much."

The Senator's position is that there was no sex of any kind, before, during or after the ride or the party. It was a completely proper weekend of relaxed and friendly fun and games to reward the six girls for their faithful service to the Kennedys. The girls were no political groupies. He was not a frisky politician on the loose and on the make. No one planned to stay overnight at the cottage for any immoral purposes.

Others point out that there were five married men without their wives, an unmarried chauffeur, and six young, unmarried girls together for four days and three nights at an isolated cottage that they had all planned to spend the night in. The nonbelievers shrug and ask, who is kidding whom?

The Senator himself noted the propriety of the situation in his television address after pleading guilty to leaving the scene of an accident:

> There is no truth, no truth whatever, to the widely circulated suspicions of immoral conduct that have been leveled at my behavior and hers regarding that evening. There has never been a private relationship between us of any kind. I know of nothing in Mary Jo's conduct on that or any other occasion — the same is true of the other girls at that party — that would lend any substance to such ugly speculation about their character. Nor was I driving under the influence of liquor.

He told the *Boston Globe* in the fall of 1974:

> Let me say that there has been a great deal of ugly speculation about the conduct of Mary Jo and myself which is completely inaccurate and completely untrue. . . . The defamation or attempted defamation of her character is one of the aspects I regret most deeply.

The other male members of the party have always steadfastly maintained the same position. For all of them it is certainly understandable, because one could hardly expect the married men's contingent to commit public suicide. Worse than facing the press, they had to face their wives.

The Senator's biographer, Burton Hersh, takes a novel line in throwing the sex angle out of the picture. He says that the Senator would not have a sexual interest in any of those homely young women. Mary Jo was pastier and tougher than the rest, and not at all the Senator's type. Hersh states that if the Senator had planned the party as an orgy, he would have gone after a higher standard of excellence. Chivalry as practiced by Mr. Hersh is not an issue.[1]

[1] Burton Hersh, *The Education of Edward Kennedy,* pp. 385-97.

Earlier in this book, however, Mr. Hersh speaks admiringly of the Senator's down-to-earth approach in his college days. When he picked up his dates, he made it clear "early and with great undisguised feeling," exactly what he expected of them. Hersh says young Edward radiated vigor and had an overabundance of the sap of health.

In his inquest findings on the Kopechne death, Judge Boyle did not believe the Senator's testimony. He reasoned that the Senator and Mary Jo were going to the secluded beach. Even the pro-Kennedy Burton Hersh has no doubt that the Senator was headed towards the deserted beach. Hersh plays it down by saying that the Senator was overwhelmed by problems, difficulties and crowds, and was going to the lonely beach in search of solitude.

If the Senator and Mary Jo left the cottage at 11:15 and were spotted by Look at 12:45, what could have happened during that hour and a half? Some of the many possibilities could explain why the Kennedy forces fought against an autopsy. It could also explain the reaction to the blood test the police reported on examining Mary Jo's blouse.

When Mary Jo's body was removed from the Senator's car, she had on a blouse, bra, and slacks — but did not have on any panties. Whether she wore any that night or misplaced them during the lost hour is a subject of speculation.

The police chemist reported that benzidine testing gave affirmative reactions for blood presence on her blouse — but not on the bra or slacks. On the blouse, the affirmative areas were the back, the backs of the sleeves and the back of the collar.

These locations seem odd areas for injury. She would have had to lie down on her back in an area of blood, attired only in the blouse, or to lean back into such an area, or to sustain injuries only to her upper back and arms to account for the stains.

What was a difficult problem became even more complicated when the flustered Dr. Mills, the Medical Examiner, and Eugene Frieh, the mortician, quickly went over Mary Jo's body and made their findings. They testified that the body had no visible signs of injury — no cuts, bruises, marks, lesions, breaks — nothing that would result in bleeding. Still, there were the unexplained blood reactions.

Kennedy backers as well as Kennedy haters have made efforts to explain the blood reactions. Backers surmise that blood came from the lungs during the drowning and ran around under water, setting into the back of the blouse. That is absurd from the start because it could not happen that way. The swirling waters within the death car negate this theory. Enemies of the Kennedys hint at violent beatings, abortions, illegal drug reactions or even the murder of Mary Jo before the car went off the bridge.

But all of these theories have one fault in common. They assume the benzidine test actually showed the presence of blood. Since the police did such a sloppy investigation of the whole affair, reporters have grabbed onto the blood tests as one of the few straws of real evidence. This is understandable. Unfortunately, they are wrong. Blood just isn't part of this case.

For corroboration let's refer to an authoritative text used widely by police departments and the courts. It is written by Professor Paul Kirk and is titled *Crime Investigation – Physical Evidence and the Police Laboratory*.[1] On pages 189 et seq., Kirk discusses the benzidine test for the presence of blood. He cautions that such testing requires close attention to the speed of color reaction development, color clarity, local or spotty results and any abnormalities in color reaction appearance.

The ability to correctly interpret test results and to avoid the many pitfalls, Kirk states, comes from experience. You just don't throw a little benzidine around and yell blood. Kirk warns anyone handling physical evidence to be very careful, because many everyday substances give positive reactions similar to blood when tested with benzidine. It requires an expert to detect the difference. Among the substances that will give a *false positive reaction* are:

> citrus fruits
> some noncitrus fruits
> many vegetables

[1] New York: Interscience Publishing, 1968.

some chemicals
oxidants
paints
green leaves
and *ordinary grass.*

If this "blood" was in fact ordinary grass stains, and no similar evidence was found on the bra and slacks, it is not difficult to picture the details of the lost hour and a half. A revised timetable will account for the time involved and the condition of the blouse. Pressure against ordinary grass on the ground would set the invisible stain. Even if the Senator admits one day that Look saw him at 12:45, he will still have to account for the lost hour and the grass stains.

THE GREAT ESCAPE

SPEEDING TOWARDS THE BEACH and bridge, afraid that the familiar Kennedy face might have been seen, Mary Jo and the Senator went off Dyke Bridge together into the darkness of Poucha Pond. Only Senator Kennedy emerged alive. For Mary Jo, the Senator's car became a wet coffin. Here is Kennedy's inquest version of what happened:

> Well, I remember the vehicle itself just beginning to go off the Dyke Bridge, and the next thing I recall is the movement of Mary Jo next to me, the struggling, perhaps hitting or kicking me, and I, at this time, opened my eyes and realized I was upsidedown, that water was crashing in on me, that it was pitch black. I knew that and I was able to get a half a gulp, I would say, of air before I became completely immersed in the water. I realized that Mary Jo and I had to get out of the car.
>
> I can remember reaching down to try and get the doorknob of the car and lifting the door handle and pressing against the door and it was not moving. I can remember reaching what I thought was down, which was really up, to where I thought the window was and feeling along the side to see if the window was closed, and I can remember the last sensation of being completely out of air and inhaling what must have been a lung full of water and assuming that I was going to drown and the full realization that no one was going to be looking for us that night until the next morning and that I wasn't going to get out of that car alive and then somehow I can remember coming up to the last energy of just pushing, pressing, and coming up to the surface.

The Senator is able to remember so many details about this short fraction of time that it is strange he can't remember how he got out of the car. It is one of the missing pieces of the Chappaquiddick puzzle that has caused much controversy.

How the Senator could possibly have gotten out alive has been the continuing source of argument and confusion. Using maps and myths, various authors have manipulated this escape to fit their theories. One author has him pulling a movie stunt-man performance by opening the door and jumping out of the car before it went off the bridge. That would sound and look great on television, but it just didn't happen that way.

Another author theorizes the Senator was alarmed that Sheriff Look might follow and question them, so he ducked out of the car and hid in the bushes while Mary Jo went on alone. She was supposed to make a swing around to the beach and back to pick him up if the police didn't follow. Being unfamiliar with his car, she drove off the bridge alone. Kennedy told part of the truth. He drove the car off the bridge, and did not jump out along the way.

Most of the reports indicate, however, that it would be just about physically impossible for a big man like the Senator — six foot two, 220 pounds — wearing a back brace, fully clothed and wedged upside down under the steering wheel in a car full of water to have worked his way around and out of the window. They refer to National Safety Council material to back up their claims, and we believe them.

The Senator has not helped because he has insisted that he has no recollection as to how he got out of the car. In his story to the police, nine hours after the accident, Kennedy said:

> The car turned over and sank into the water and landed with the roof resting on the bottom. I attempted to open the door and window of the car but have no recollection of how I got out of the car.

In his television speech, the Senator added some more details that came to mind as his shock wore off:

> . . . The car that I was driving on an unlit road[1] went off a

---

[1] The Senator's continual reference to the "unlit road" has prompted many to ask whether his physical condition that night prevented him from noticing if his head lights were on or off, since car lights illuminate dark roads.

narrow bridge which had no guardrails and was built on a left angle to the road.[1] The car overturned in a deep pond and immediately filled with water. I remember thinking as the cold water rushed in around my head that I was for certain drowning. Then water entered my lungs and I actually felt the sensation of drowning. But somehow I struggled to the surface alive.

Many reporters have jumped on this part of his somewhat selective amnesia to say that if he can't remember getting out, then he didn't and was thus not in the car when it hit the water. This has prompted a lot of theories. They back up their claims by pointing out that little Mary Jo, not much over a hundred pounds and unencumbered by any steering wheel, could not get out of the two completely open windows on her side.

There is no real contradiction involved in the Senator getting out of the car while Mary Jo was trapped inside — the physical facts of the accident left no other possibility. You have to think the accident through.

Senator Kennedy's car went off the bridge in a rolling turn and half flip. It hit on the passenger side and top with such force that it dented the top, cracked the windshield, and blew in both of the passenger side windows. As it slowly filled with water, the car toppled over and settled down into the pond with the wheels up on the surface, pointing back towards the direction from which it had come.

Try it yourself with a model car and you will wonder how all the experts missed it. The car landed with the passenger windows hitting the water. The open window on the driver's side is an upright escape hatch. The driver is almost forced out of it. The incoming water through the blown passenger windows below would actually help. There is an appreciable time for the driver to get out before the car fills up with water and settles to the bottom. The car didn't hit the water and sink

---

[1] "A consultant's report done for his 1969 defense concluded that because of the road terrain and the contour of the bridge, which bears sharply to the left midway across, braking only will not prevent a car in this position, traveling at a speed of 20 m.p.h., from going over the rail. Braking at the edge of the bridge would stop the car in 33 feet, the report said, and Kennedy's car went over the rail at 18 feet." *The Atlanta Constitution,* October 27, 1974.

like a stone — air had to first be displaced as it completed the slow toppling turn. The trunk and car still had air in them nine hours later.

Just close your eyes and picture it. As the car was going down on its passenger side, Senator Kennedy's open window was his escape hatch. Depending on the time of the accident, his window could have been above the pond's surface by between eight and 22 inches. At low tide, the water depth was only five or six feet; Kennedy's Oldsmobile 88 was six feet, eight inches wide.[1] Senator Kennedy had enough time to climb out before the car came to a rest, top down, on the bottom of Poucha Pond.

For the Senator there is life . . . for Mary Jo there is slow waiting for death. Water is pouring in both windows on her side. She can't push out against the force of the incoming water and she can't reach the Senator's escape hatch because he is standing on top of her. No wonder he testified that he remembered Mary Jo struggling and perhaps hitting or kicking him — so would you if a man was standing on you in a sinking car. Her struggles probably helped push him out.

Thus, the Senator's escape is a combination of fate, the roll of the car and his natural urge to survive. Mary Jo's submerged tomb is a combination of fate, the roll of the car and Kennedy's nine-hour silence.

---

[1] Between 11:00 and midnight, it was a dead low tide. Around 12:45 the tide was up. The car would have still landed and toppled slowly over in the same way, but the water would be around six to seven and one half feet deep, still allowing for the same method of escape.

RESCUE TALES

IN SENATOR KENNEDY'S first statement to the police, ten hours after the accident, he said:

> I came to the surface and then repeatedly dove down to the car in an attempt to see if the passenger was still in the car. I was unsuccessful in the attempt.

> I was exhausted and in a state of shock. I recall walking back to where my friends were eating. There was a car parked in front of a cottage and I climbed into the back seat. . . . I then asked someone to bring me back to Edgartown.

In his television speech, one week later, the Senator added more details:

> . . . I made immediate and repeated efforts to save Mary Jo by diving into the strong and murky current but succeeded only in increasing my state of utter exhaustion and alarm. . . . Instead of looking directly for a telephone after lying exhausted in the grass for an undetermined time, I walked back to the cottage where the party was being held and requested the help of two friends, my cousin Joseph Gargan and Paul Markham, and directed them to return immediately to the scene with me — this was some time after midnight — in order to undertake a new effort to dive down and locate Miss Kopechne. Their strenuous efforts, undertaken at some risks to their own lives, also proved futile.

Six months later, Senator Kennedy shed some light on the extent of his "shock" which prevented him from seeking professional help for Mary Jo:

Q. And you were fully aware at that time of what was transpiring?

A. Well, I was fully aware that I was trying to get the girl out of that car and I was fully aware that I was doing everything I possibly could to get her out of the car. . . .

Q. You were not confused at that time?

A. Well, I knew there was a girl in that car and I had to get her out. I knew that.

Q. But there was no confusion in your mind about the fact that there was a person in the car and that you were doing the best you could to get that person out?

A. I was doing the very best I could to get her out.

The greatest moral taint of the whole Chappaquiddick case is the fact that Senator Kennedy left Mary Jo in the car for over nine hours — while he claims he was in shock and doing his "very best" to help her.

Having escaped a wet death, Senator Kennedy probably did not go back in after Mary Jo. As you will see, this whole sad truth slowly unfolds. Once out of the car, and rested from his escape, Kennedy said at the inquest: "I went back to the road and I started down the road and it was extremely dark and I could make out no forms or shapes or figures, and the only way that I could even see the path of the road was looking down the silhouettes of the trees on the two sides and I could watch the silhouette of the trees on the two sides and I started going down that road walking, trotting, jogging, stumbling as fast as I possibly could." Senator Kennedy was asked if he passed any houses with lights on, and he replied, "Not to my knowledge; I never saw a cottage with a light on."

Some say the Senator ran in fear and secrecy back to the cottage to get Gargan and Markham. They quote the Bible saying the guilty flee where no man pursueth. Many non-believers say that in his panic, Kennedy could see only one safe cottage in his mind. Although just 100 feet from the Dyke

Bridge was the Malm house with a light on, he passed it by. He also passed four other visible cottages, each of which had a telephone. Across the street from the party cottage is the volunteer fire station with a glowing red light and unlocked door, ready 24 hours a day. Was it foremost in Senator Kennedy's mind, as Jack Anderson says, to get the ". . . always-willing Gargan to take the bad publicity for running the Oldsmobile off the bridge?"[1]

At the inquest, here is what the Senator says happened next:

Q. And when you arrived at the cottage . . . did you speak to anyone there?

A. Mr. Ray LaRosa.

Q. And what did you tell him?

A. I said, get me Joe Gargan.

Q. Did you go inside the cottage?

A. No, I didn't go inside.

Q. What did you do? Did you sit in the automobile at that time?

A. Well, I came up to the cottage, there was a car parked there, a white vehicle, and as I came up to the back of the vehicle, I saw Ray LaRosa at the door and I said Ray get me Joe and he mentioned something like right away, and as he was going in to get Joe, I got in the back of the car.

Q. And now, did Joe come to you?

A. Yes, he did.

Q. And did you have a conversation with him?

A. I said, you had better get Paul too.

---

[1] Jack Anderson, "Washington Merry-Go-Round," September 25, 1969.

Q.   What happened after that?

A.   Well, Paul came out, got in the car. I said, there has been a terrible accident, we have got to go and we took off down the road, the Main road there.

Q.   How long had you known Mr. LaRosa prior to this evening?

A.   Eight years, ten years, eight or ten years.

Q.   Were you familiar with the fact that Mr. LaRosa had some experience in skin diving?

A.   No, I never did.

Q.   And what happened after the three of you arrived there?

A.   Mr. Gargan and Mr. Markham took off all their clothes, dove into the water and proceeded to dive repeatedly to try to save Mary Jo.

Q.   Now, do you recall what particular time this is now when the three of you were at the —

A.   I think it was at 12:20, Mr. Dinis. I believe that I looked at the Valiant's clock and believe that it was 12:20.

As in much of the Senator's testimony, there is a little problem with the time element here. This time he is way off, because the rented Valiant *had no clock*. Chrysler Corporation officials say that "this particular model (100) does not offer a clock as factory installed equipment." *Time* magazine (10-7-74) examined the Valiant and "discovered no drill holes, dashboard scratches nor any other indications that the car had ever had a clock."

Each time the Senator told his version of what happened that night, more details were added. His simple, one-page statement to the police on the morning of the accident was expanded to several dozen pages of inquest testimony. Cynics say that since the Senator is so adept at adding details with each rendition of the story, if given the opportunity to run it through a few more times, he might wind up saving Mary Jo and thus end all discussion of the case.

Kennedy, Gargan and Markham probably did return to the accident scene, but it is doubtful that Gargan or Markham did any diving. The very tight time element that Sheriff Look's testimony holds them to alone rules out such efforts. It must be remembered that the first Kennedy story made *no mention* of any such heroics by his two loyal friends.

The time schedule is very important here. Senator Kennedy has listed his actions and the amount of time each took with two limits in mind. The first is that he has based his sworn testimony on leaving the cottage at 11:15 to catch the ferry. The second comes later, but he talked with the owner of the Shiretown Inn at 2:25 a.m. to supposedly find out the time. To keep a plausible story, the Senator has timed his schedule to fit perfectly between these two limits:

11:30 p.m.	Senator Kennedy and Mary Jo have left the cottage, and driven off the bridge.
11:50	Kennedy claims to have spent 20 minutes trying to rescue Mary Jo.
12:10 a.m.	He spent 20 minutes resting on shore.
12:25	Kennedy took 15 minutes walking back to the cottage.
12:35	He got Gargan and Markham and they drove back to the bridge.
1:20	Gargan and Markham spent 45 minutes trying to rescue Mary Jo again.
1:30	They gave up, took 10 minutes to drive to ferry slip.
1:40	They talked on the ferry slip for approximately 10 minutes.

2:00   It took Kennedy approximately 20 minutes to swim to Edgartown, rest on shore and stagger to his room at the Shiretown Inn.

2:25   He paced back and forth in his room until he went downstairs in clean, pressed clothes to ask the manager of the Shiretown Inn what time it was and to complain of some noise that was disturbing him.

It is amazing how well he is able to accurately fit his schedule together when he was in such shock throughout that night. Though he could not remember how he got out of the car, his sense of timing is perfect.

If Kennedy did leave at 11:15 and spent an hour and a half with Mary Jo somewhere, here is how the time schedule fits in with Sheriff Look spotting him at 12:45 a.m.:

12:50   Kennedy drove off the bridge.

1:10   He spent 20 minutes trying to rescue Mary Jo.

1:30   Kennedy spent 20 minutes resting.

1:45   Walked back to cottage — 15 minutes.

2:05   Got Gargan and Markham, drove back — 10 minutes.

2:50   Gargan and Markham spent 45 minutes trying to rescue Mary Jo.

3:00   Got into car and drove to ferry slip — 10 minutes.

3:10   Got out of car, talked at ferry slip — 10 minutes.

3:30   Kennedy swam to Edgartown, rested, staggered to Shiretown Inn — 20 minutes.

3:55   Rested, paced and went to complain and find out that the time was 2:25.

The Senator's story just doesn't fit; there are too many added events to fill up his time. A more realistic time schedule is:

11:15	They left the cottage to be alone.
12:45	Spotted by Deputy Look.
12:50	Drove off the bridge.
1:00	Kennedy had escaped from the car.
1:30	Kennedy had rested and gone to cottage.
1:40	He got Gargan and Markham, the three of them returned to the bridge but quickly left to get Kennedy off the island.
2:00	They found a boat and went to Edgartown.
2:25	Kennedy dressed and went down to establish an alibi time with the owner of the Shiretown Inn.

We will go into all the details about finding a boat and establishing an alibi in the next several chapters, but first we must deal with why we do not believe that Kennedy, Gargan or Markham made any rescue attempts. The time element clearly rules them out. Again, it must be remembered that the first Kennedy story made no mention of any heroic rescue attempts made by his two friends.

The public did not find out about the new rescue efforts until a week later in his television speech which was not under oath. Kennedy thought that all legal proceedings were behind him, and did not anticipate the inquest six months later. Thus, all the added details had to be worked into his inquest testimony and enlarged upon.

Kennedy added the news of Gargan's and Markham's heroics, because they had been criticized by many, including Theodore Sorensen, for failing to report the accident. They had no claim to shock.

Like the Senator, both were attorneys. There had even been

talk of bringing criminal charges against them. Senator Kennedy explained this withholding of information to the *Boston Globe* in 1974: "I felt that I was going — not going to bring them any further involvement which I considered my problem and my responsibility and my obligation. Let me say at this time that that was a mistake and I certainly should have included their names in that (police) report. I intended to do them a favor, and I'm afraid I did them a disservice."

Many publications have expressed doubt and outright disbelief that the Senator went back into the water to try and save Mary Jo. Even Walter Steele, that very friendliest of prosecutors, didn't believe it. When you add the heroics of his two friends, though they may sound good, they don't hold water. None of the girls reported noticing that either Gargan or Markham were wet and exhausted, even though Senator Kennedy said Gargan "was scraped all the way from his elbow, underneath his arm was all bruised and bloodied." They both came in soaked, exhausted, and wounded, yet no one noticed anything unusual at this sober, clock-watching party.

At the inquest six months later, the Senator was well over his shock from his "cerebral concussion" and was able to add more details. He testified to somehow getting out of the car, shocked and confused, and being swept away by the swift current. He was able to get back to the car by swimming and wading. However, if the accident occurred at the time the Senator stated, there was no current to sweep him away — it was a dead low tide. Chappaquiddick's low tide began to turn at 9:45 p.m. Friday evening. Witnesses the next morning calculated the exact low tide time and placed it between 11:00 and 11:30, when the water was extremely shallow and calm. The Senator contradicts his own sworn testimony on the accident time by specifying that the current was strong.

There is an even more damning statement in the inquest record by Paul Markham. No one at the inquest followed up on this statement. Apparently no one caught it until now. In testimony about how the three of them returned to the accident scene, Markham quoted the Senator as saying:

He said, "I thought for sure I was going to die." He said he somehow got out of the car. He tried to go back into the water again to see if he could get Miss Kopechne or try to open the door or do something. He said he couldn't. He said the only thing he could think of was to come back and get us (Gargan and Markham) to see if we could help.

Read the two main sentences again:
HE TRIED TO GO BACK INTO THE WATER AGAIN TO SEE IF HE COULD GET MISS KOPECHNE OR TRY TO OPEN THE DOOR OR DO SOMETHING. HE SAID HE COULDN'T.

Couldn't what? Couldn't go back into the water again? Couldn't face that black, swirling current he said had almost killed him? That he went back into the water again but couldn't help?

You make the decision. In making it, remember that in each of the Senator's three statements he claims that he made "immediate" efforts by diving to save Mary Jo as soon as he surfaced — he never talks of leaving the water and coming back. Once out of the car and safely on the shore, did Senator Kennedy go back and attempt to save Mary Jo, or did he dash away to save his political life? You decide.

LEANDER SWIMS THE HELLESPONT

HOW SENATOR KENNEDY got back to Edgartown is a mystery. By his own timetable he should have bumped into Jared Grant who had held the ferry open late waiting for him. In the Senator's first statement to the police, he said:

> I recall walking back to where my friends were eating. There was a car parked in front of a cottage and I climbed into the back seat. . . . I then asked someone to bring me back to Edgartown.

Since the police asked him no questions, and his first statement didn't give the answer, no one knew how he had got back. For a week, the only information was, "I then asked someone to bring me back to Edgartown." Did they get him back by boat, plane, ferry, or did they swim him across? It's not likely that, as one reporter theorized, Senator Kennedy walked across the water.

He might have still been in shock that morning when he signed the first confession, because after a week with his advisors, it all became clear. Senator Kennedy told a national television audience:

> Instructing Gargan and Markham not to alarm Mary Jo's friends that night, I had them take me to the ferry crossing. The ferry having shut down for the night, I suddenly jumped into the water and impulsively swam across, nearly drowning once again in the effort.

At the inquest, Senator Kennedy testified:

> You take care of the girls, I will take care of the accident, — that is what I said and I dove into the water. Now I started to swim

out into that tide and the tide suddenly became, felt an extraordinary shove and almost pulling me down again and suddenly I realized at that time even as I failed to realize before I dove into the water that I was in a weakened condition, although as I had looked over that distance between the ferry slip and the other side, it seemed to me an inconsequential swim; but the water got colder, the tide began to draw me out, and for the second time that evening I knew I was going to drown and the strength continued to leave me. By this time I was probably 50 yards off the shore and I remembered being swept down toward the direction of the Edgartown Light and well out into the darkness, and I continued to attempt to swim, tried to swim at a slower pace to be able to regain whatever kind of strength that was left in me. And some time after, I think it was about the middle of the channel, a little further than that, the tide was much calmer, gentler, and I began to get my — make some progress, and finally was able to reach the other shore and all the nightmares and all the tragedy and all the loss of Mary Jo's death was right before me again.

Many people question why Senator Kennedy failed to include this swim in his first police statement. Gargan and Markham come off looking callous both in their concern for Mary Jo and for their exhausted Senator. They have told two different stories. One is that they went in the water to try to bring the Senator back, and the other is that they knew he could swim the channel several times a day, both ways, fully clothed and with a back brace on — so they weren't concerned. Lack of worry about a man in shock from a serious accident does not describe two loyal friends. Why didn't they call the Shiretown Inn or the police station to see if he had made it safely to the other side? Did their physical condition from the party or their alleged rescue attempts prevent them from using the phone at the ferry slip?

Perhaps the answer is that they were not telling the truth and were instead more worried about the Senator's political future than anything else. Jack Anderson says: "The Senator's two loyal friends hustled him by boat off the island so he could establish an alibi at the Shiretown Inn, away from the scene of the accident. It now appears that Markham remained at the inn with the Senator and Gargan returned to the Chappaquiddick cottage."[1] Whether Markham stayed with the Senator all night and worked on his alibi ultimately does not change the question of how the Senator got back to Edgartown or the other issues involved here.

Though Senator Kennedy claims he swam back to Edgartown, that is probably a product of his own press releases and a week of high-pressure advice at Hyannis Port. They could not very well say he took a boat across, because the question would produce the trap of "Where did you get the boat, and how did you think to look for it if you were in shock?" If he said he didn't remember, then all the critical fingers would point to Gargan and Markham who would then be entrapped and possibly forced to discredit much or all of the Senator's story.

Again, the facts are against the Senator. A Mr. Ballou from Rhode Island saw three men crossing the Edgartown Channel in a boat at 2:00 a.m. Gargan and Markham told the party girls that they had been looking for a boat. A boy on the island said his boat had been used during the night and tied up in another place. These facts were known by authorities and never used against Senator Kennedy.

This whole boat report makes sense and is consistent with the Senator's action that night. Everything fits into place except the stories told by the Senator. His versions are like wrong pieces slipped into a jigsaw puzzle box. If an alibi were being planned, then it was important to get Gargan back to the island and accident scene, and the Senator far removed from the death car — back to his hotel to establish an alibi time with the owner of the Shiretown Inn at 2:25. It was the Kennedy loyalty test put into action. Senator Kennedy was known to test his friends by demanding: "If I committed (some offense or outrage), you'd take the rap for me, wouldn't you?" The evidence points towards Gargan being ready to pass the test for several hours, while Mary Jo was left in the submerged car and Kennedy was in his rooms establishing an alibi.

[1] Jack Anderson, "Washington Merry-Go-Round," September 26, 1969.

DIAL-A-PRAYER

ONCE BACK at the Shiretown Inn, Senator Kennedy testified at the inquest: "I went to my room and I was shaking with chill. I took off all my clothes and collapsed on the bed, and at this time I was very conscious of a throbbing headache, of pains in my neck, of strain on my back, but what *I was even more conscious of is the tragedy and loss of a very devoted friend.*" (Emphasis added.) The Senator continued:

> I was unable to really determine, detect the amount of lapse of time, and I could hear noise that was taking place. It seemed around me, on top of me, almost in the room, and after a period of time, I wasn't sure whether it was morning or afternoon or nighttime. . . .

Though he was conscious of the loss of Mary Jo, his mind was flying off in wild hallucinations; time, noise and events were throbbing in and out of his room like whirling dervishes — like the mesmerized visions of the sorrow (and whatever) induced DT's of a broken man . . . a potential presidential candidate.

Kennedy said at the inquest: ". . . I put on some dry clothes that were there, pants and a shirt, and I opened the door and I saw what I believed to be a tourist, someone standing under the light off the balcony and asked what time it was. He mentioned to me it was, I think 2:30, and went back into the room."

During that long night following the accident, Senator Kennedy's mind was supposedly fogged by panic. Though he was able to run and get his friends Gargan and Markham, he was unable to call the police. Certain events were clear, others were blocked by his "cerebral concussion" and "shock". Kennedy even theorized that it all happened because ". . .some

actual curse did actually hang over all of the Kennedys."
In his first statement to the police, Senator Kennedy said:

> I remember walking around for a period of time and then
> going back to my hotel room. When I fully realized what had
> happened this morning, I immediately contacted the police.

In his television speech, he said:

> In the morning, with my mind somewhat more lucid, I made
> an effort to call a family legal advisor, Burke Marshall, from a
> public telephone on the Chappaquiddick side of the ferry and
> belatedly reported the accident to the Martha's Vineyard
> police.

To the *Boston Globe*, in the fall of 1974, Kennedy explained
further his failure to report the accident:

> By the time that I arrived on the other shore, I was absolutely
> spent. Absolutely exhausted. And just saying 'I just can't do it. I
> just can't do it. I just can't do it.' I remember walking up
> towards the Shiretown Inn and walking through the front
> entrance and just going up to my room. . . . My conduct was
> irrational and indefensible and inexcusable and inexplicable
> . . . but it was a mental state of mind. . . .

His somewhat selective amnesia is questioned by most
people. They point out that Senator Kennedy only fills in the
gaps where it helps his case. His own doctor applied the
made-to-order diagnosis of a "slight concussion" — take a
pencil and rap yourself on the head; medically, you have just
suffered a "slight concussion".

Kennedy knew what he had to do, but backed down saying,
"I just can't do it." In further comments to the *Boston Globe*,
Kennedy actually admitted that the idea of using the phone
had penetrated his mental fog: "I was overcome by the possibilities of and the requirements of calling Mrs. Kopechne
and telling her of the loss of her daughter and calling my
parents — my mother and father — as well as my wife. . . ."

It seems logical that if he knew there were certain "requirements" he had to do for Mary Jo who lay dead or

drowning in his car, then it seems he was not so completely lost in shock. Many feel that he was more concerned with the Kennedy name and his political future than with notifying the police or the Kopechnes about Mary Jo. Just one phone call from the Senator would have changed history. He would have changed from an unstable Presidential candidate to a Presidential hero. All it would have taken was one call. His supporters would have done the rest.

Actually, the Senator and/or his associates made at least 17 calls during that night while he was in shock, but none to report the accident.[1] Perhaps the following record will help the Senator's understandably faulty memory.

A very worried Senator Kennedy made five calls before leaving Chappaquiddick Island and twelve when he reached the Shiretown Inn. All 17 were billed to Kennedy's credit card number through the Edgartown operator.[2] More could have been made and either paid for, charged to another credit card or placed collect.

Although Kennedy has denied making these calls, it would have been to his advantage to have the phone company release his records if he was telling the truth. Hanify, one of his lawyers, was the Director of the New England Telephone Company and could surely have overcome any possible red tape.

While Mary Jo lay trapped in his car, Kennedy's first call lasted 21 minutes; he called the family compound in Hyannis Port. Remember, Senator Kennedy said, "I was overcome by the possibilities of and the requirements of . . .calling my parents — my mother and father — as well as my wife. . . ." It had always bothered him that his parents had heard about the assassinations of his two brothers over the radio and wanted to personally warn them.

The second call was to his alter ego, Ted Sorensen. The telephone company records show he spoke about something for eight minutes with Sorensen in New York City.

[1] Information on the phone calls obtained from reporter Arthur Egan in *Human Events*, August 23, 1969, and Jack Anderson, "Washington Merry-Go-Round," August 22, 1969.

[2] Why wasn't the telephone operator questioned? Surely she would have remembered the calls.

The third call went to his attorney, Burke Marshall, in the Washington, D.C. area. The records show that Marshall failed to answer, and Kennedy would call again later that morning. The fourth call was to his own unlisted number in Boston. While still on the island, he made a fifth call, to Sorensen in New York.

These five calls do not indicate shock. They indicate a desperate man trying to get advice and give warning about a political firestorm approaching. One must figure that each person he spoke with either called other Kennedy loyalists or made plans to aid the Senator. None of them tried to aid Mary Jo. Even a long distance, anonymous call to the Edgartown police could possibly have saved her life.

If the plan of action was to get the Senator off the island, as Jack Anderson reported, then he must have decided to use the phone at the inn, because 12 more calls were made from the pay phone there. He was coherent and appeared normal to the Shiretown Inn receptionist, who spoke with him two and a half hours before he called the police. He borrowed a dime from her to make another call.

Reporter Arthur Egan said, "It was noted by the persons who secured the list of 17 calls, that there were no efforts to reach police, fire or Coast Guard officials to summon help to learn the fate of Miss Kopechne." Some say the Senator acted quite rationally — by calling the police he would be admitting knowledge and involvement.

These calls were not surprising revelations to the authorities. Police Chief Dominick Arena — who earned the nickname of "Whitewash" from reporters — ". . . has acknowledged that he was well aware of the phone calls. Reporters who have kept close tabs on the incident, moreover, stress that Arena's threat to produce the calls at a pre-trial hearing, shoot down Teddy's 'shock' story, caused Teddy to change his mind and plead guilty to leaving the scene of an accident rather than face a hearing and possible trial."[1] Jack Anderson concluded, "These calls uphold my story that Kennedy wasn't stumbling around in confusion but was trying to extricate himself."[2]

[1] *Human Events*, August 23, 1969.
[2] Jack Anderson, "Washington Merry-Go-Round," August 22, 1969.

The fact that the authorities did not use this information should in no way affect its unquestioned authenticity. The traffic court prosecution for leaving the scene is what is known as a "sweetheart arrangement."[1]

[1] Should this whole case be called Dikegate, Chappagate or outrageous? One reporter said the only difference between Nixon's and Kennedy's scandals was that Kennedy pardoned himself.

DOA — NINE HOURS LATER

THERE REALLY IS no middle ground in the Chappaquiddick case. Either you believe Senator Kennedy was shocked into another world, or you do not believe he told the truth. Evidence is limited by the wall of silence erected by the Kennedy forces. The *Boston Globe* investigation of the Senator in 1974, five years after the accident, "was thwarted throughout by Kennedy loyalists who could have shed light on the events leading up to the Kopechne death. Thus, nine of the ten members of Kennedy's entourage refused to answer *Globe* questions, and the Senator refused to urge any to cooperate with the probe."[1]

If the Senator was not in shock but was callously planning his moves, what was the purpose? Waiting nine hours could not help any story. The answer of many is that the Senator was planning an alibi. Jack Anderson and many others will state this is a fact. The *Boston Globe* quoted a highly reliable source on the reason for the nine-hour delay and his outward calmness the next morning before he reported to the police: "Joseph Gargan had agreed the night before to take responsibility for the accident, making it necessary for Kennedy to appear unaware of the tragedy. 'It's clear (the source stated) that Kennedy later decided the alibi either couldn't work or he couldn't live with it.' "

If he was planning an alibi — which seems logical from the evidence — then it certainly would explain his calm and unworried appearance to all who saw him Saturday morning. If he wasn't the driver of the car, then he would not have known about what happened after he left the party and thus would appear unworried. The idea here is that he planned to

[1] *Human Events,* November 9, 1974.

act out third-party pain over the death of Mary Jo. It would be a kind gesture for him to handle all the arrangements for Mary Jo's grief-stricken parents.

Think about it, and also consider what Kennedy told the police on Saturday:

> When I fully realized what had happened this morning, I immediately contacted the police.

Remember these two contradicting ideas when you read further.

At 7:30 a.m. Senator Kennedy was dressed in spiffy boating clothes and ready to race again that afternoon. Chief Arena described his appearance: "He had a white sport shirt on, short sleeves and a pair of blue slacks, and he looked neat. He looked physically okay. . . ."[1] Kennedy ordered several newspapers from the Shiretown Inn desk clerk and appeared quite normal when he borrowed a dime for a phone call.

Senator Kennedy bumped into Ross Richards, the winner of Friday's regatta. They spent a leisurely fifteen minutes discussing Friday's race and the upcoming one that afternoon. The Senator gave every indication that he intended to race. He appeared normal. At 7:50 a.m. Stanley Moore and Mrs. Richards joined them in the open courtyard to discuss the regatta. They chatted about everything except Mary Jo, because Senator Kennedy had not ". . .fully realized what had happened this morning."

Meanwhile, two fishermen landed the biggest fish story of their lives. Around 8:00 a.m., Bob Samuel, 22, and Joseph Cappavella, 15, saw the car sticking above the surface of Poucha Pond. Since they did not know if anyone was trapped inside, and were not in shock, they immediately went for help. They ran to the Malm house right next to the bridge, and had Mrs. Malm call the police.

By this time, Gargan and Markham joined the Senator at the Shiretown Inn. How they crossed from Chappaquiddick to Edgartown is a mystery, because the ferry operator said he didn't take them. Think back upon the boat and alibi, unless of

[1] Jack Anderson, "Washington Merry-Go-Round," September 2, 1969.

course you believe they also swam across. If there was such an alibi being planned, were doubts forming in the Senator's mind? Probably.

At the inquest, Senator Kennedy said:

Q. After that noise at 2:30 in the morning, when did you first meet anyone, what time?

A. It was sometime after 8:00.

Q. And you met whom?

A. Sometime after 8:00, I met the woman who was behind the counter at the Shiretown Inn and I met Mr. Richards and Mr. Moore, very briefly Mrs. Richards, and Mr. Gargan and Mr. Markham, and I saw Mr. Treter . . .

Q. Now, what time did Mr. Gargan and Mr. Markham arrive?

A. About a few — I would think about 8:30, just a few minutes after I met Mr. Moore probably.

Q. Did you have any conversation with Mr. Markham or Mr. Gargan or both at that time?

A. Well, they asked, had I reported the accident, and why I hadn't reported the accident; and I told them about my own thoughts and feelings as I swam across the channel and how I had always willed that Mary Jo still lived; how I was hopeful even as that night went on and as I almost tossed and turned, paced that room that night that somehow when they arrived in the morning that they were going to say that Mary Jo was still alive. I told them how I somehow believed that when the sun came up and it was a new morning, what had happened the night before would not have happened and did not happen, and how I just couldn't gain the strength within me, the moral strength to call Mrs. Kopechne at 2:00 in the morning and tell her that her daughter was dead.

So, while the car had been discovered, Senator Kennedy was still unable to gain the "moral strength" to call the authorities.

He lost his personal battle for self-control and the strength to face his responsibilities. Not all men are perfect, but this is a serious defect which could threaten the security of the United States and the world if a President ran from a decision in fear and panic.

Around 8:30 a.m., Edgartown Police Chief Arena arrived at the accident scene. He borrowed some swimming trunks and had a very difficult time reaching the car. The current was so strong that he could not make any dives to see if anyone was inside.

Kennedy told him later in his statement: "I came to the surface and then repeatedly dove down to the car in an attempt to see if the passenger was still in the car." In his television speech, Senator Kennedy said: "I made immediate and repeated efforts to save Mary Jo by diving into the strong and murky current but succeeded only in increasing my state of utter exhaustion and alarm."

That morning, the current was quite swift. Chief Arena — a powerful swimmer without a brace, soggy clothes or in a state of shock — could hardly get to the auto without being pulled away by the current. It was a millrace — the same type of current that had swept under the bridge around 12:45 a.m. the night before. Arena was just able to sit on the car and wait for the scuba diver. He told the others on shore not to even put a boat out, because the current would pull it away. Chief Arena was able to read the license plate and had one of his assistants on shore radio it in for owner identification. Deputy Sheriff Look positively identified it as the car he had seen at 12:45. A search of the shoreline for other bodies was started.

Chief Arena put out a call for John N. Farrar, storekeeper and navy-trained captain of the Scuba, Search and Rescue Division of the Edgartown Volunteer Fire Department. He was in his bait and tackle shop when he received the call about 8:30. Farrar immediately went to the fire station for his diving gear and was joined by another fire department member.

They both drove to the ferry and crossed. Antone Silva, the fire chief, was already waiting for them on the Chappaquiddick side. From there, the fire chief drove them directly to Dyke Bridge — about 3 miles. During that short drive, Farrar put on his scuba gear to save time.

They arrived at the accident scene at approximately 8:45 and Farrar was immediately in the water. Chief Arena had made it to the car, but was just sitting on the rear because the current had been too strong for him.

Farrar submerged and first checked the driver's side, but could see nothing. He then made his way around to the rear of the car and saw Mary Jo's feet through the back window (the car was upside down). Hoping to save her life, he quickly entered the car through one of the broken out windows on the passenger side. He found Mary Jo in the back seat. Her head was cocked back, and her face was pressed upward into the foot well. Her hands were still grasping the edge of the back seat — she was trying to take advantage of the last bit of air. Farrar found she was dead and believes "she died of suffocation in her own air void. But it took her at least three or four hours to die."

Farrar gives the following reasons for believing Mary Jo was trapped alive:

First, the way the car entered the water, which would have caused it initially to trap a large amount of air.

Second, the position of the car on the bottom. It was resting on the hood ornament and the brow of the windshield, with the rear end just slightly below the surface of the water.

Third, the consciously assumed position of the victim, as previously described.

Fourth, the fact that air bubbles emanated from the car as it was removed from the water 10 to 11 hours after the accident was said to have happened, and

Fifth, the fact that there was a large air void and a lack of water in the trunk of the car when it was removed.

He quickly mentions several recent accidents where people have survived up to six hours in submerged cars. It's a chilling thought — what could have been and should have been.

After a quick, ten-minute examination of Mary Jo's body, Dr. Mills pronounced that she was "the most drowned person

I've ever seen." Though his description gained as much detail at the inquest as his timetable of death dissolved, he insists that with "just light pressure on the chest wall. . .water would simply pour out of the nose and mouth."

Standing right next to Dr. Mills when he made these observations was Eugene Frieh, the undertaker. Frieh did not see any great outpouring of water. He said, "It produced some water flow, water and foam, mostly foam." He later added, "Very little water was expelled from the lungs . . . I expected much more water."

In Dr. Mills' own copy of the *Handbook for Massachusetts Medical Examiners* the general autopsy guidelines are stated:

(1) If you are wondering whether you should do an autopsy or not, you had probably better do one. . . .

(2) Deaths occurring following motor vehicle accidents should be autopsied if there is any question as to whether the accident caused the death.

Dr. Mills was criticized heavily within the medical profession for his decision against an autopsy of Mary Jo's body.

Mary Jo could possibly have been in the early stages of pregnancy, and Dr. Mills was the first to find that she had no panties on under her slacks. Yet he ruled out an autopsy. Dr. Sidney Weinberg, medical examiner of Suffolk County, New York, was quoted as saying that "autopsies were required in his jurisdiction for all victims of automobile accidents. 'When you have a young woman of child-bearing age, you are doubly suspicious,' and the body is examined for signs of pregnancy and criminal abortion."[1]

Dr. John Edland, former medical examiner for Monroe County, New York, said: "It's a real farce to bring the body of a dead girl out of a car after nine hours and have someone make a pronouncement that it is a routine drowning." Dr. Lester Adelson, forensic pathology professor at Western Reserve Medical School, said that an autopsy would have stopped "all kinds of ugly rumors and speculations. There is everything to

[1] *Human Events,* November 2, 1974.

gain and nothing to lose by performing an autopsy in a case of this kind."[1]

If Dr. Mills had ordered the standard autopsy, then there would be no question of how or approximately when Mary Jo died. An autopsy could have only served the purpose of truth. Instead, we are left with the recurring vision of Mary Jo alone, waiting in the black, wet darkness for help.

[1] *Human Events*, November 2, 1974.

OLD HOME WEEK

MARY JO WAS DEAD, and the authorities knew of the accident. But Kennedy had not yet reported the accident. Before he could bring himself to face the police, he needed more advice. At the inquest, he said he went back to Chappaquiddick Island that morning, ". . . to make a private phone call to one of the dearest and oldest friends that I have and that was Mr. Burke Marshall. I didn't feel that I could use the phone that was available, the public phone that was available outside of the dining room at the Shiretown Inn, and it was my thought that once I went to the police station, that I would be involved in a myriad of details and I wanted to talk to this friend before I undertook that responsibility." To talk privately with this friend, Senator Kennedy bypassed thirty to forty other phones in Edgartown. Some say that he finally gave up his alibi when he reached Chappaquiddick Island that morning around 9:00 a.m.

While at the ferry slip using the phone, Senator Kennedy saw a hearse head towards Dyke Bridge. Someone then informed him that his car had been involved in an accident, and that a young girl was dead. Either he or Markham said, "We just heard about it." Perhaps the hearse made him "fully realize" what had happened, because instead of rushing to the scene of the accident, he took the ferry back to the police station.

By this time, Chief Arena knew that the car belonged to Senator Kennedy, and, hesitantly, he called his office to have Kennedy quietly found. The Senator, already waiting for him at his office, would speak to no one but Arena about the accident.[1] So the Chief hurried back to the station in his wet bathing suit.

It certainly was more convenient for the Senator to meet at the station, because he was using the Chief's private office, desk and phone. The Senator was not under arrest and had already made several phone calls. Kennedy had Policewoman Carmen Salvador dial several of these calls. From what she overheard, none of the calls made sense; they all seemed to be part of continued conversations. What Kennedy never admitted was that they *were* continuations — of some of the 17 earlier calls made by him or made on his behalf. The calls are logical, considering what was at stake for the Senator.

One of the most important calls Senator Kennedy made from the Chief's phone was to order one of his aides to remove Mary Jo's body from the island and the jurisdiction of Massachusetts. *This was done before he had spoken in person with the police chief!* There had been *no investigation* or *established cause of death* that he could have known about, yet he ordered his aide to bring a death certificate. The Senator came out of his shock rather quickly.

Kennedy later told the *Boston Globe*, "I was overcome by the possibilities of and the requirements of calling Mrs. Kopechne and telling her of the loss of her daughter." Whatever factors had made this call only a "possibility" were now removed. From the Chief's phone the Senator called the Kopechnes and broke down during the conversation. The Kopechnes had lost a daughter, but many of Kennedy's supporters said he stood to lose much, much more.

The Senator spoke a few words to the Chief, but was asked no questions. While the Senator and Markham set to work to outline a story of what happened, the other members of the party made plans to leave the island. Markham wrote out the confession in long hand, Kennedy read it over to see if it was correct, and the Chief typed it up. Though Senator Kennedy was bound by law to answer all questions and truthfully tell what had happened, his statement raised more questions than it could ever hope to answer.

[1] Chief Arena knew the Senator from the days when Arena had been on duty at the State House as a driver and had chauffeured Kennedy from the State House to the airport.

Senator Kennedy's original confession copy vanished from the Chief's office — following the style of the whole unusual "investigation." The text of Senator Kennedy's statement is below. When it was first released, it did not contain Mary Jo's name, because Kennedy did not know how to spell it.

> On July 18, 1969, at approximately 11:15 p.m. on Chappaquiddick Island, Martha's Vineyard, I was driving my car on Main Street on my way to get the ferry back to Edgartown. I was unfamiliar with the road and turned right onto Dyke Road instead of bearing left on Main Street.
>
> After proceeding for approximately one-half mile on Dyke Road, I descended a hill and came upon a narrow bridge. The car went off the side of the bridge. There was one passenger with me, Miss Mary Jo Kopechne, a former secretary of my brother, Robert Kennedy.
>
> The car turned over and sank into the water and landed with the roof resting on the bottom. I attempted to open the door and window of the car but have no recollection of how I got out of the car.
>
> I came to the surface and then repeatedly dove down to the car in an attempt to see if the passenger was still in the car. I was unsuccessful in the attempt.
>
> I was exhausted and in a state of shock. I recall walking back to where my friends were eating. There was a car parked in front of the cottage and I climbed into the back seat.
>
> I then asked someone to bring me back to Edgartown. I remember walking around for a period of time and then going back to my hotel room. When I fully realized what had happened this morning, I immediately contacted the police.

In this statement there are many contradictions and errors. Kennedy was not unfamiliar with the road, and it was not 11:15 when they turned onto Dyke Road. He did not attempt to rescue Mary Jo, and made no mention of any heroic attempts by Gargan and Markham. The confession gave no indication of how he got back to Edgartown, or of his many phone conversations in the morning, or of how he planned to race Saturday afternoon while he was still in shock.

Kennedy said, ". . . I descended a hill and came upon a narrow bridge." However, this hill is more like a bump, and is 670 feet from Dyke Bridge. It drops only one foot per hundred, so he hardly "descended a hill." From all appearances, it is a perfectly straight, flat approach to the bridge. In his inquest testimony, Senator Kennedy said: "I would estimate that time to be a fraction of a second from the time that I first saw the bridge and was on the bridge." This seems rather odd. Car headlights pick up the bridge 400 feet away. A driver in normal condition would have to really try hard if he wanted to run off the bridge.

Senator Kennedy told the Chief not to release his statement until he had talked with his lawyer. This instruction was to allow time to control or make corrections in what appeared to be a confession. He also knew that if his statement was released while he was still on the island, the members of the press — who had already started to gather — would ask him some questions for which he was not prepared.

The Chief had no objections. Everything seemed under control. Kennedy was going to his family stronghold at Hyannis Port and would get back in touch with him so that they could quickly settle the whole matter. It seemed to be an open and shut case. Cynics say that the Chief left all the back doors open, and Senator Kennedy shut them in the public's face.

Prosecutor Walter Steele arrived and spoke with Kennedy and Markham in confidence, because he had known them both. Since Kennedy wanted to get off the island quickly, Steele went with Markham to the Shiretown Inn so he could grab some clothes. They discussed the case at length. Steele told them they would have no problem with him. The wheels of justice seemed to be spinning backwards.

WHO'S WHO REPORTS FOR DUTY

BY THE TIME SENATOR KENNEDY had "fully realized what had happened," and before he went to the police, the remains of the party had been cleaned up. All signs of liquor had been taken and spread around the Chappaquiddick dump. Local authorities decided that a standard autopsy would not be necessary, so a Kennedy aide prepared the death certificate for the body to be taken off the island. The five surviving girls were flown away without answering a single official question.

Chief Arena and the local authorities thoughtfully arranged Senator Kennedy's departure so that he could avoid the press. Escaping out the back door of the police station, state officials drove him to the airport where they had arranged for Edgartown's Democratic leader, Bob Carrol, to fly him straight to Hyannis Port.

When Senator Kennedy arrived at his family stronghold Saturday afternoon, his family and advisers were faced with what appeared to be a damaging confession. The Kennedy machine had its work cut out. Carloads of what some call "Teddy Hacks" poured into the compound, "taking every spare bed," as *Time* reported. The Kennedy estate was absorbing the Camelot Who's Who of the World. On the surface it was absurd to bring this list of VIP's together over a simple traffic accident. Their real mission, however, was to salvage their potential Presidential candidate.

Reporting for duty to help the Senator explain his conduct were:

Robert McNamara	President of the International Bank, Secretary of Defense under President Kennedy,

	President of the Ford Motor Company.
Theodore Sorensen	Editor, Author *(Kennedy)*, Special Assistant (speechwriter) to President Kennedy.
Richard Goodwin	Lawyer, Special Assistant to President Kennedy.
Burke Marshall	Former Assistant U.S. Attorney General under Robert Kennedy.
John Culver	U.S. Congressman.
Judge R. Clark	Lawyer, former District Court Judge in Massachusetts.
Robert Clark, III	Lawyer, son of the foregoing.
Sargent Shriver	Kennedy brother-in-law, Ambassador, Peace Corps, U.S. Vice-Presidential Candidate in 1972. Announced Presidential Candidate for 1976 (this may be a holding action for Ted, as Shriver will withdraw if necessary, as is expected of those who marry into the Kennedy family).
Frank O'Conner	Kennedy assistant.
Paul Markham	Lawyer, former U.S. Attorney for the State of Massachusetts.
Milton Gwirtzman .	Lawyer and speech writer.
John Tunney	U. S. Congressman.
David Burke	Lawyer, Edward Kennedy's Administrative Assistant.

Many others showed up, including Lamoyne Billings,

Stephen Smith, David Hackett, Frank Mankiewiez, Joseph Gargan and Richard McCarran. There was also phone contact with many Kennedy followers, including Senator Abraham Ribicoff, John Kenneth Galbraith and Arthur Schlesinger, Jr. Perhaps Prosecutor Steele and Chief Arena should have been there, but it appeared that they were doing their very best for the Senator in Edgartown.

First they drew up a battle plan: Avoid the press, come up with a plausible story, negotiate the best possible court arrangement for the Senator, write a heart-rending national address and then — refuse to discuss the issue. It was to be a real blitzkrieg. They wanted to bury the issue with the victim before the contradictions dawned on the American public.

Presidents have declared war with less advice and fewer advisors. This has to be one of the greatest gatherings of big-time talent ever brought together to advise one man. All Kennedy was charged with was leaving the scene of an accident, a simple police court offense. While they argued and debated strategy, the Senator spent his time crying, drinking, sailing and flying kites. After a week, when their mission was accomplished, they folded their tents and crept away. If they had all been charging fees, even the Kennedy fortune would have felt the strain.

THE DOUBLE STANDARD

WHILE THE PRESS howled over Edgartown and Hyannis Port for any bits of information, the Edgartown police were waiting for some signal on what to say and do.[1]

On Tuesday, July 22, at 9:30 a.m., funeral services were held for Mary Jo at St. Vincent's Catholic Church in Plymouth, Pennsylvania. Senator Kennedy arrived with a neck brace on. It was a dramatic move that backfired. Many of the press knew that since the accident he had been seen flying kites and sailing, so they were satisfied that the Senator had a selectively painful neck. For the rest of the week, he wasn't seen with it on.

After some anxious days, Steele and Arena were contacted by the Kennedy forces. Two attorneys representing the Senator — Judge R. Clark and his son — arranged a secret meeting with the Prosecutor and Police Chief some miles into the woods to avoid public knowledge of what would appear to be questionable circumstances.

At this secret meeting on Wednesday the 23rd, they agreed — subject to approval from Hyannis Port — that the Senator would plead guilty to leaving the scene of the accident. Steele would then recommend the minimum sentence and arrange for it to be immediately suspended.

Early the next day, in an empty room at the airport, they wrapped up the guilty plea deal. Hyannis Port had given the go ahead.

At this meeting, they also agreed to change the court hearing date from Monday, the 28th, back to Friday, the 25th. Publicly, they said the change was necessary for security. Most

[1] Reporters weren't the only ones digging for facts on this story. Nixon dispatched the plumbers to get some dirt on his potential 1972 opponent.

likely they switched dates to avoid a full-scale trial that would have probably developed Monday. Kennedy could not give his television speech until after the court proceedings, and his advisors knew it was essential to get the Kennedy line across to the nation before the public had a full weekend to react to rumors and theories.

With the authorities in line, the security details were extended. They planned the best way to keep the Senator one step ahead of the press and any questioning. Everything was designed to protect and convenience the Senator during his ordeal.

Steele and Arena worked and reworked their end of the Hyannis Port to protect the Senator. As if trying to find a Judas or Dean in their midst, they swore everyone to secrecy. This included the entire Edgartown ten-man police force, a crew of deputy sheriffs, two policewomen, extra bailiffs, courtroom assistants and a contingent of state policemen.

Late Thursday night, Prosecutor Steele, Arena, and the defense attorneys all met again secretly to check out last minute details. They wanted no surprises. The Kennedy attorneys helped the Chief edit his 'statement of facts' to be given to the court. As planned, Steele had filed his accident report that Thursday afternoon, before any real investigation was started or completed. The Kennedy team was in complete control.

On Friday, Kennedy arrived to face the music. Delivered safely to the courthouse, he quickly pleaded guilty. Steele recommended the lowest sentence allowed by law, and that it immediately be suspended. To add icing to the cake, Steele told the judge — with no basis in fact — that at the time of the accident the Senator was driving with "extreme care". Steele later refused to let Scripps-Howard reporter Dan Thomasson see the public record supporting such a statement. Steele had Thomasson thrown out.

The probation officer announced to the court that Senator Kennedy had no prior record of any kind, but unaccountably he was not struck down by lightning. As we will see, the Senator had quite a collection of traffic violations in various jurisdictions. Perhaps the probation officer meant there was no prior record of Kennedy having driven off Dyke Bridge.

After the guilty plea, there were to be no embarrassing questions or inconvenient examination of the Senator. Though Kennedy took at least nine hours to report the accident, Steele assured the court that the Senator had not tried to conceal his identity.

Judge Boyle imposed the recommended sentence, after receiving assurance from Richard McCarran — Town Attorney for Edgartown and the court counsel for Kennedy recommended by Prosecutor Steele — that a suspended sentence was acceptable to Senator Kennedy.

With the legal proceedings over, Senator Kennedy was whisked out of the courthouse by the back door to avoid the press. Under a police escort, he was taken to the airport and flown to Hyannis Port. Good timing, attention to detail and close cooperation had seen poor Teddy through his ordeal. Earlier, Kennedy had told Chief Arena that they must handle the matter right to "avoid criticism." Perhaps this was what he meant all along.

Senator Kennedy's recent statement criticizing the Nixon pardon comes to mind:

> "Do we operate under a system of equal justice under law? Or is there one system for the average citizen and another for the high and mighty?"

The reaction of many was, "Is this boy for real?" I'm sure that when the Massachusetts Judiciary heard this statement, they arose and stood with bared and bowed heads while they murmured "Amen."

THE PRIOR RECORD

ALTHOUGH THE PROBATION OFFICER in Edgartown had access to the facts, he incorrectly stated that the Senator had no prior record. Actually, Kennedy had a long prior record of arrests related to driving offenses.

Throughout the late 1950's, Kennedy's driving habits and hot-rod attitude got him into trouble. Here is a part of the record he compiled at the University of Virginia:

> In March 1957, Kennedy was arrested for speeding and fined $15 by the Albemarle County Court.

> In June 1958, he was again picked up for speeding and again ordered to pay a $15 levy.

> Also in June 1958, the young Kennedy was arrested for "reckless driving — racing". He was fined $35 plus court costs.

> In December 1959, Kennedy was arrested for failure to stop for a red light, convicted and fined $10 plus court costs.[1]

Lt. T. M. Whitten of the Albemarle County Police reports that Kennedy had sped through town at 90 miles an hour several times. Whitten had tried to follow Kennedy in an earlier chase, but lost him at the end when Kennedy turned off his lights. Two nights later, Whitten saw him speed through the same red light and gave chase. This time he knew where the race would end and was able to follow closely. Kennedy tried the same light cutting trick, but Whitten found his car and the young Kennedy hiding on the seat. Kennedy was charged and convicted. "There was a minor effort to

[1] *Human Events,* August 2, 1969.

suppress the incident, charged Whitten, but no one knows who was responsible. Whitten remarked the case was simply '. . .shelved. They kept it quiet for too damn long,' he said."[1]

There are other reports of drunken driving and wild romantic rides, but verification is difficult. There is even the unpublicized report of the Senator hitting a child and, although he was not at fault, leaving the scene — only to be forced back by his companions. The fact is that Senator Kennedy did have a prior record which the probation officer should have and could have known. His driving was so bad that the Senator had been using chauffeurs almost exclusively for some years.

[1] *Human Events*, August 2, 1969.

THE SELLING OF AN ACCIDENT

THE SENATOR HAD FACED the law and admitted his guilt to a charge many said did not fit the accident. Edgartown authorities were relieved that they had finally put a lid on the case, many were outraged and felt that justice had not been served. The Kennedy PR machine quickly set to work to win back any lost followers. The Kennedy forces must have believed that all was behind them; they didn't count on any attempts to exhume Mary Jo's body for a belated autopsy, or on the inquest six months later.

The national television speech was all set. The word was passed down, through union ranks and Kennedy ward supporters, to turn out a large positive response. This was to show the world that the people believed his story — a cleansing of this latest Kennedy tragedy. Then, at 7:30 Friday night July 25, the nation watched Senator Kennedy reveal that he was finally "free to tell what happened." No one questioned whether he had not also been free to tell what happened a week earlier. The speech was aimed at the sympathy nerve of the nation; its arrows penetrated deeply.

As the Senator spoke, people realized that what they thought had happened after reading his police confession had not actually been the whole story. Many new details appeared. Senator Kennedy neither explained the discrepancies between his two statements nor concentrated on the actual events. He loaded the speech with trivia — much as he would at the inquest.

In this speech, the Senator omits all mention of his half hour boating chit-chat and how he was so in shock that he was actually planning to race Saturday afternoon. Perhaps he intentionally forgot to mention all those minor events, knowing how the nation would react. To convince the undecided,

Senator Kennedy dug up brothers John and Robert along with Webster, Sumner and Lodge — everyone except Mary Jo for the standard autopsy which would have cleared up most of the doubts.

Remember, none of the following is part of the official record nor was the speaker under oath. Here is the Kennedy story — some say the whole story — and some say nothing but a story:

My fellow citizens:

I have requested this opportunity to talk to the people of Massachusetts about the tragedy which happened last Friday evening. This morning, I entered a plea of guilty to the charge of leaving the scene of an accident. Prior to my appearance in court it would have been improper for me to comment on these matters. But tonight I am free to tell you what happened and to say what it means to me.

On the weekend of July 18, I was on Martha's Vineyard Island participating with my nephew, Joe Kennedy — as for thirty years my family has participated — in the annual Edgartown sailing regatta. Only reasons of health prevented my wife from accompanying me.

On Chappaquiddick Island, off Martha's Vineyard, I attended on Friday evening, July 18, a cookout I had encouraged and helped sponsor for a devoted group of Kennedy campaign secretaries. When I left the party, around 11:15 p.m., I was accompanied by one of these girls, Miss Mary Jo Kopechne. Mary Jo was one of the most devoted members of the staff of Senator Robert Kennedy. She worked for him for four years and was broken up over his death. For this reason, and because she was such a gentle, kind and idealistic person, all of us tried to help her feel that she still had a home with the Kennedy family.

There is no truth, no truth whatever, to the widely circulated suspicions of immoral conduct that have been leveled at my behavior and hers regarding that evening. There has never been a private relationship between us of any kind. I know of nothing in Mary Jo's conduct on that or any other occasion —

the same is true for the other girls at that party — that would lend any substance to such ugly speculation about their character. Nor was I driving under the influence of liquor.

Little over one mile away, the car that I was driving on an unlit road went off a narrow bridge which had no guardrails and was built on a left angle to the road. The car overturned in a deep pond and immediately filled with water. I remember thinking as the cold water rushed in around my head that I was for certain drowning. Then the water entered my lungs and I actually felt the sensation of drowning. But somehow, I struggled to the surface alive. I made immediate and repeated efforts to save Mary Jo by diving into the strong and murky current but succeeded only in increasing my state of utter exhaustion and alarm.

My conduct and conversations during the next several hours, to the extent that I can remember them, make no sense to me at all. Although my doctors informed me that I suffered a cerebral concussion as well as shock, I do not seek to escape responsibility for my actions by placing the blame either on the physical, emotional trauma brought on by the accident, or on anyone else. I regard as indefensible the fact that I did not report the accident to the police immediately.

Instead of looking directly for a telephone after lying exhausted in the grass for an undetermined time, I walked back to the cottage where the party was being held and requested the help of two friends, my cousin Joseph Gargan and Paul Markham, and directed them to return immediately to the scene with me — this was some time after midnight — in order to undertake a new effort to dive down and locate Miss Kopechne. Their strenuous efforts, undertaken at some risks to their own lives, also proved futile.

All kinds of scrambled thoughts — all of them confused, some of them irrational, many of them which I cannot recall and some of which I would not have seriously entertained under normal circumstances — went through my mind during this period. They were reflected in the various inexplicable, inconsistent, and inconclusive things I said and did, including such questions as whether the girl might still be alive somewhere out of that immediate area, whether some awful curse did actually hang over all the Kennedys, whether there was some justifiable reason for me to doubt what had happened and to delay my report, whether somehow the awful weight of this incredible incident might in some way pass from my shoulders. I was overcome, I'm frank to say, by a jumble of emotions — grief, fear, doubt, exhaustion, panic, confusion and shock.

Instructing Gargan and Markham not to alarm Mary Jo's friends that night, I had them take me to the ferry crossing. The ferry having shut down for the night, I suddenly jumped into the water and impulsively swam across nearly drowning once again in the effort, and returned to my hotel about 2:00 a.m. and collapsed in my room. I remember going out at one point and saying something to the room clerk.

In the morning, with my mind somewhat more lucid, I made an effort to call a family legal advisor, Burke Marshall, from a public telephone on the Chappaquiddick side of the ferry and belatedly reported the accident to the Martha's Vineyard police.

Today, as I mentioned, I felt morally obligated to plead guilty to the charge of leaving the scene of an accident. No words on my part can possibly express the terrible pain and suffering I feel over this tragic incident. This past week has been an agonizing one for me and the members of my family, and the grief we feel over the loss of a wonderful friend will remain with us the rest of our lives.

These events, the publicity, innuendo and whispers which have surrounded them and my admission of guilt this morning, raise the question in my mind of whether my standing among the people of my state has been so impaired that I should resign my seat in the United States Senate. If at any time the citizens of Massachusetts should lack confidence in their Senator's character or his ability, with or without justification, he could not in my opinion adequately perform his duty and should not continue in office.

The people of this state, the state which sent John Quincy Adams and Daniel Webster and Charles Sumner and Henry Cabot Lodge and John Kennedy to the United States Senate, are entitled to representation in that body by men who inspire their utmost confidence. For this reason, I would understand full well why some might think it right for me to resign. For me, this will be a very difficult decision to make.

It has been several years since my first election to the Senate. You and I share many memories — some of them have been glorious, some have been very sad. The opportunity to work with you and serve Massachusetts has made my life worthwhile.

And so I ask you tonight, people of Massachusetts, to think this through with me. In facing this decision, I seek your advice and opinion. In making it, I seek your prayers. For this is a decision that I will finally have to make on my own.

It has been written a man does what he must in spite of personal consequences, in spite of obstacles and dangers and pressures, and this is the basis of all human morality. Whatever may be the sacrifices he faces, if he follows his conscience — the loss of his friends, his fortune, his contentment, even the esteem of his fellow man — each man must decide for himself the course he will follow. The stories of past courage cannot supply courage itself. For this, each man must look into his own soul.

I pray that I can have the courage to make the right decision. Whatever is decided and whatever the future holds for me, I hope that I shall be able to put this most recent tragedy behind me and make some further contribution to our state and mankind, whether it be in public or private life.

Thank you and good night.

The planned reaction poured in. Massachusetts — and much of the nation — responded on cue. The press was a little smarter. After reading the speech to learn "what happened", they realized they'd been had and continued the outcry for the truth.

The speech itself is *Grade A Ham*. The Senator was more concerned with melting hearts than with giving the public the truth so that it could make an intelligent judgement. After hearing the speech, Sorensen, who had just completed his book, *The Kennedy Legacy*, deleted the references he had made to "Teddy's bright promise."

Part Two

Justice Obstructed

DEATH OF AN AUTOPSY

IN AUGUST, with a better-late-than-never attitude, Edmund Dinis, the District Attorney of the Southern District of Massachusetts, petitioned the State of Pennsylvania authorities to have Mary Jo Kopechne's body exhumed for an autopsy—after the body had left the island, after the Senator had pleaded guilty to a lesser charge and after his television speech. To many, Dinis appeared to be playing both sides of the fence.

Dinis petitioned the Pennsylvania authorities in Luzerne County so that an autopsy could be performed in accordance with the laws of the State of Massachusetts.[1] He said he wanted to determine the cause and circumstances of her death, as it was the subject of official inquiry in the southern district of Massachusetts.

Normally the request from a sister jurisdiction to help carry out official duties would bring some degree of cooperation. In this case Dinis received anything but cooperation—he got a hard time from everyone, including Mary Jo's parents, the Kennedys, all their lawyers, and the Pennsylvania authorities—specifically District Attorney Blythe Evans of Luzerne County and his honor, Judge Bromiski. They all treated Dinis as though he were a criminal defendant trying to defeat justice instead of an official trying to solve a crime. Dinis never had a chance. It was like the Edgartown authorities all over again.

Dinis had no one but himself to blame for his autopsy troubles. While the body was in Edgartown it had been subject

[1] As stated in the *Handbook for Massachusetts Medical Examiners:* "(1) If you are wondering whether you should do an autopsy or not, you had probably better do one . . . . (5) Death occurring following motor vehicle accidents should be autopsied if there is any question as to whether the accident caused the death."

to his control. But somehow he let it get away from him. Reasons for that slip are various, complicated, confused and contradictory. There have been so many allegations, explanations and denials of why no autopsy was set up by Dr. Mills—who conducted some sort of quickie, ten-minute, on-the-scene examination—that the truth is long lost. It can only be said that the handling of this charade, whether purposeful or accidental, was a new high in official stupidity that has yet to be explained.

An autopsy could have cleared away much of the mystery that still surrounds the death of Mary Jo. It would have prevented or anticipated a lot of the whisperings and rumors that persist to this day. An autopsy could have made helpful findings such as that death did or did not occur by poisoning, strangulation or manual suffocation, among other forms of homicide. It could have forever laid to rest or confirmed any talk of pregnancy. It would certainly have established whether Mary Jo had sexual relations before death. An autopsy could have disposed of these and many other questions. The Senator had everything to gain and nothing to lose... *if* he was telling the truth.

While Edgartown officialdom may have muffed the autopsy ball that weekend, the Kennedy team didn't miss a trick. They moved in sharply, smartly and efficiently. The presidency was at stake. They took over, and they took.

Fortunately for the Senator, one of the things he did while in shock early Saturday morning "before he fully realized what had happened . . . and immediately notified the police" was to phone an aide on his staff and give instructions for the moving of Mary Jo's body off the island and out of the state to Pennsylvania. What an irony that this call was made from the office of Police Chief Arena while the Chief was helping to get the body out of the Senator's car in Poucha Pond. Give the Senator credit. Once he came out of his panic, he didn't miss a shot—he touched every base.

Don Gifford responded to the Senator's call and arrived in Edgartown Saturday afternoon of the accident. He went directly to the office of Dr. Mills with an undertaker and a death certificate at about 2:00 p.m. While the town people and the press were still asking what happened, Gifford told Dr. Mills the name of the decedent and had him sign the death certificate. Dr. Mills was ready and willing. An unwilling participant in this case, he just wanted everyone to leave him alone.

Gifford was ready to take the body off the island immediately in a chartered plane, but even the Kennedys couldn't change the weather. The secret departure was delayed until Sunday, when the shroud-wrapped body—they had no coffin—was taken away from the scene of the accident and out of the state of Massachusetts, while officials in Edgartown were still wondering whether or not there should be an autopsy. This is the background on which the Pennsylvania courts will decide whether Mary Jo's body will be exhumed for an autopsy as requested by Massachusetts authorities.

An autopsy is a post-mortem examination, a necropsy, an official examination of a body after death, with such dissection as necessary in exposing vital organs in order to determine the cause of death. The practice exists in every state in the Union. It is routine, not automatic, in cases where there are reasonable grounds to believe death may have been caused by unlawful means, or where the cause of death is not known. Chappaquiddick is a case in point.

However, Judge Bromiski had different thoughts on when, or if, to have an autopsy. He said to exhume the body and have an autopsy, it not only must be reasonable and have good cause, but there also had to be an "urgent necessity" clearly established. He said the law reaches into the grave in "only the rarest of cases," and even then only if "clearly necessary" and not unless there is "a strong showing that the facts sought (to show crime) will be established." By the time you get through meeting these 'standards' set up by the good Judge, you don't need an autopsy—you have enough evidence to hang everybody in sight without an autopsy.

Now, let's see what the law books say in this area. The coroner, the man who presides at this sort of business, is no johnnie-come-lately. If you wish to read some of the historical background on the office, see the case of *Gavagan v Marshall*, 33 Southern 2d, 862, where the Florida Supreme Court discourses learnedly on this office—which was first established in England in 1194.

The laws of inquest are to be liberally construed, as the purpose is to protect the public and not the criminal. Inquest determines the cause of death and detects crime. An autopsy must be held if there is reasonable ground to believe death was caused by unlawful means. Any doubts are in favor of and not against holding such an examination. When the autopsy is authorized by law (even *required* as in this case) it is presumed to be proper. To prevent such autopsy, it must be shown that it would be of no value, ineffectual or unnecessary. If the coroner does not hold an inquest in a proper case, it is the *duty of the court* to have the body exhumed and an autopsy performed. (See *18 Corpus Juris Secundum* 292 et seq.; *18 American Jurisprudence* 2d, 521; *48 American Law Reports* 1209 et seq.)

It seems that Pennsylvania law would also require an autopsy here (see *Frick v McClelland* 122 Atlantic 2d, 43, decided by the Pennsylvania Supreme Court in 1956) and that the approval of the Kopechnes was not required (p. 45). It is repeated that the purpose of inquests and autopsies is to *protect the public* and not the criminal. This is the law in all states, including Pennsylvania—with the possible exception of Luzerne County where Judge Bromiski presided.

Despite what the law says about all of this, here is what Judge Bromiski had to say:

> Even if we assume that an autopsy would reveal a *broken neck* or any other bone in the body, a *fractured skull, the rupture of an internal organ,* none of these would be incompatible with the manner in which this accident occurred. (emphasis added)

Are these possible revelations part of death by drowning? The Judge added:

> To consider any other cause of death at this time would give loose rein to speculation unsupported by any medical facts of record.

This is Bromiski's Catch 22. Massachusetts requested the autopsy to establish the medical facts, yet the judge dismissed their petition because it was unsupported by any medical facts! That's like saying you have to perform an autopsy to establish the grounds for the requested autopsy. What more could the Kennedy team have hoped for?

In making his ruling, Judge Bromiski was also giving the back of his hand to the intent of Section I of Article IV of the Constitution of the United States. This requires that the several states must give "... full faith and credit ... to the public acts, records and judicial proceedings of every other state." This wasn't just another law suit. The petitioners were officials of the state of Massachusetts, advising the state of Pennsylvania that an autopsy was required in connection with official proceedings then pending in Massachusetts.

While Judge Bromiski was burying Dinis along with Mary Jo, Robert W. Nevin, the Medical Examiner of Dukes County, Massachusetts, jumped the Dinis ship. Though he had officially joined in the petition for the autopsy, he suddenly joined the Kennedy anti-autopsy group by withdrawing his request without notice to Dinis. He had seen the handwriting on the wall; he had gone over to the winning side, the Kennedy side.

Senator Kennedy was holding all the cards, and now he showed his famous compassion. After all hopes for an autopsy were ended, the Senator noted that Mr. and Mrs. Kopechne had opposed the autopsy request and said he was happy about the Judge's ruling because of what it would mean for them.

Why did the Kopechnes oppose an autopsy here? Mrs. Kopechne has publicly stated she told Mr. Dinis they would consent if he would tell them there was evidence of foul play (criminality), but Dinis either could not or would not. And this conduct by Mr. Dinis is inexplicable because even Judge Boyle, backpedaling as fast as he was able, later came up with criminal misconduct.

The opposition by the Kopechnes was a 'must' for the Senator, as he had no legal standing to oppose the request for autopsy aside from the obvious fact that such a course of action by him would have been political suicide. So in addition to the negative action by Dinis, the Kennedys had lined up the biggest gun available. On behalf of the Senator there appeared on the scene in Wilkes-Barre, Pennsylvania, no less a personage than His Eminence (the late) Richard Cardinal Cushing, one of the foremost Churchmen in the United States and a longtime intimate friend of the Kennedys. He called on the Kopechnes and advised them it was their Christian duty to oppose the efforts to exhume the body and perform an autopsy. He said they must do all in their power to prevent such a desecration of their daughter's body.

So the Kopechnes retained Joseph Flanagan of Wilkes-Barre to appear before Judge Bromiski on their behalf. Mr. Kopechne took the stand and testified they were against any autopsy, they saw no value in one and it would be like another funeral.

It is not known by what arguments the Kennedy forces persuaded Cardinal Cushing to go to the Kopechnes, but Teddy had benefited by the Cardinal before. In his 1962 campaign for the Democratic Senatorial Nomination, one of Teddy's publicity props was a picture of the Cardinal and himself; his opponent Eddie McCormack yelled foul.[1]

---

[1] Victor Lasky, *J.F.K. The Man and the Myth*. New York: The MacMillan Company, 1963.

JUDGE BROMISKI'S OPINION

JUDGE BROMISKI'S DENIAL of the petition for exhumation and autopsy of Mary Jo Kopechne is included here as part of the record. His holding appears clearly contrary to the well-settled law in this area. We have cited the law and included his opinion, so you can judge for yourself. You don't have to be a lawyer to make this decision[1]—you only have to be able to read. Bromiski's ruling helped Senator Kennedy cover up the truth in Mary Jo's shallow grave.

---

[1] But let your lawyer read this and tell you about it if you wish. If your lawyer agrees with Judge Bromiski, you need a new lawyer.

IN RE: KOPECHNE : IN THE COURT OF
COMMON PLEAS OF
LUZERNE COUNTY — CRIMINAL

PETITION FOR
EXHUMATION :
AND AUTOPSY

: NO. 1114 of 1969.

DECISION

This matter comes before the court upon petition and the amended petition for exhumation and autopsy of the body of Mary Jo Kopechne. The petitioners are Edmund Dinis, District Attorney for the Southern District of Massachusetts, and Robert W. Nevin, M. D., Medical Examiner for Dukes County, Massachusetts. The amended petition sets forth the following allegations of fact:

1. The death of Mary Jo Kopechne on July 18 or 19, 1969.
2. Her burial in Larksville, Luzerne County, Pennsylvania.
3. A search on July 19, 1969 which resulted in the recovery of the body of Mary Jo Kopechne from a submerged car off Dykes Bridge, Edgartown, Dukes County, Massachusetts.
4. A determination by Dr. Mills that the death of Mary Jo Kopechne was caused by asphyxiation from immersion (i. e. drowning); that the cause of death was determined without benefit of autopsy; that Dr. Mills did not perform an autopsy because he found no external signs of violence or foul play; that the body of the deceased had been submerged eight hours before his observation; that it was assumed Mary Jo Kopechne was not only the driver of the car, but was its sole occupant; and that death occurred five to eight hours prior to 9:30 A.M.
5. That the operator of the motor vehicle in which the deceased's body was found did not report the accident to the police until approximately ten hours after he said it occurred; that said operator reported that the accident happened at 11:15 P.M. on July 18, 1969; that there is a witness who claims to have seen the car at 12:40 A.M. on July 19, 1969, with two or possibly three persons in it.
6. That said operator pleaded guilty to a motor vehicle law infraction.
7. That the report of the accident made to the Chief of Police of Edgartown, Massachusetts by the operator on July 19, 1969, dif-

fered from a report of the accident broadcast by the operator on July 25, 1969.

8. That the broadcast and police reports are silent on many important details.

9. That persons who were not directly involved in the accident but who were cognizant of it, did not call the authorities.

10. That there appear on the white shirt worn by the deceased "washed out" stains that give a positive benzidine reaction, an indication of the presence of residual traces of blood.

11. That there was present a certain amount of blood in both the deceased's mouth and nose which may or may not be inconsistent with death by drowning.

12. That the information in paragraphs 10 and 11 (5-I and 5-J) was not available to the petitioners until after interment.

13. That the public interest and proper administration of justice requires confirmation of Dr. Mills's original determination of the cause of death which can be accomplished only by an autopsy.

14. The passage of time from the date of death on July 18 or 19, 1969, has not diminished to any significant degree the findings which could be made from an autopsy conducted at the present time.

15. There is now pending in Dukes County, Massachusetts, an inquest into the death of Mary Jo Kopechne.

The petitioners also allege, although they are mostly conclusions of law, the following:

16. That the purpose of the inquest is to determine whether or not there is any reason sufficient to believe that the sudden death of Mary Jo Kopechne may have resulted from the act or negligence of a person or persons other than the deceased.

17. That in order that the circumstances of death be clearly established and the doubt and suspicion surrounding the death be resolved, an exhumation and autopsy will be required.

18. That once Dr. Mills's determination of the cause of death is confirmed by an autopsy, the inquest can proceed with certainty that Mary Jo Kopechne's death was caused by drowning. However, if the autopsy should disclose that her death resulted from some cause other than drowning, the inquest may then proceed in the direction appropriate in light of the information thus revealed.

19. That in either event, an autopsy would further serve the public interest and promote the proper administration of justice in that it will disclose either the presence or absence of other conditions beside the cause of death having a critical bearing on the events and circumstances culminating in the death of Mary Jo Kopechne.

20. That the public interest in general and the proper administration of justice in particular require that all facts relative to the inquest be established with the utmost attainable degree of certainty.

The basic law on this subject was cited on pages 2 and 3 of the court's decision in this matter dated October 9, 1969. Since its applicability is equally cogent to the present matter, it is again cited:

> Courts have never hesitated to have a body exhumed where the application under the particular circumstances appeared reasonable and was for the purpose of eliciting the truth in the promotion of justice.

> On the other hand, an application for disinterment for the purpose of performing an autopsy should not be granted where there is no basis or justification for an order. Disinterment for the purpose of examination or autopsy should not be ordered unless it is clearly established that good cause and urgent necessity for such action exist. An order should not be made except on a strong showing that the facts sought will be established by an examination or autopsy. In the search for the truth, the problems of religion, the wishes of decedent, the sensitivities of loved ones and friends, or even the elements of public health and welfare, should not be disregarded. The law will not reach into the grave in search of the facts except in the rarest of cases, and not even then unless it is clearly necessary and there is reasonable probability that such a violation of the sepulchre will establish that which is sought.

The positive criteria in law are then that the application for exhumation and autopsy:
1. Must be reasonable under the circumstances.
2. Its purpose is to elicit the truth in the promotion of justice.
3. It must be clearly established that:
    (a) good cause and
    (b) urgent necessity
        for such action exist.
4. There must be a strong showing that the facts sought will be established by an exhumation and autopsy.
5. That the law will reach into the grave in:
    (a) Only the rarest of cases and
    (b) not even then, unless clearly necessary, and

(c) where there is a reasonable probability that such a violation of the sepulchre will establish that which is sought.

Let us now turn to the facts established at the hearing on the petition for exhumation and autopsy.

Essentially, they must be examined in two categories. First, from the purely legal point of view as they obtain to the eliciting of the truth in the promotion of justice and the good cause and urgent necessity that must exist to warrant an exhumation and autopsy; and, second, from the medical-legal aspect that there must be a strong showing that the facts sought will be established by an autopsy and the reasonable probability that the violation of the sepulchre will establish that which is sought.

As to the former, we are obviously referring to such facts as would cause one in authority to conclude that the death of Mary Jo Kopechne resulted from a cause other than drowning.

A review of the record of testimony, in light of the allegations of the petition from Edmund Dinis, reveals that there is some question as to whether the vehicle in question departed the Dyke Bridge at about 11:15 P.M., July 18, 1969, or about 12:40 A.M., July 19, 1969. That the driver of the vehicle failed to report the incident until some ten hours after it happened. That the report given by the driver to the Edgartown police varied from his broadcast on July 25, 1969, and that the police report and broadcast are silent on many important details of the accident. That persons not directly involved in the accident, who were cognizant of it, did not call the authorities. That there were washed-out stains on the back of the blouse of the deceased which, when exposed to a benzidine test, indicated the presence of blood and that there was present a certain amount of blood in both the deceased's mouth and nose which may or may not be inconsistent with death by drowning. That a witness saw the car in question July 19, 1969 at about 12:40 A.M. in which there appeared to be a man and a woman in the front seat and a person or a sweater or pocketbook or something on the back seat and that this car stopped and, upon approach by the witness, left hurriedly and that this was the same car that was found in Poucha Pond off the Dyke Bridge the following morning. That the witness also saw two other unidentified girls and a man that night near the scene. That there is an inquest now pending in Edgartown, Massachusetts, and that an autopsy is necessary to resolve the circumstances surrounding the death of Mary Jo Kopechne.

Starting with the premise that the purpose of this autopsy is to establish the cause of death of Mary Jo Kopechne, are there any credible facts of record here that could objectively cause one to conclude that a reasonable probability exists that the cause of death was other than death by drowning?

Let us first consider the fact that the driver failed to report the accident until ten hours after it occurred. Disposition of same need not be considered here since the Massachusetts authorities have accepted the driver's plea of guilty to leaving the scene of the accident. Furthermore, the fact that the vehicle operated by the driver may have entered the water at 12:40 A.M., July 19, 1969, rather than at 11:15 P.M., July 18, 1969, does not suggest a cause of death other than death by drowning.

Reference is then made to the difference between the driver's broadcast and the police report. Essentially, there are but two basic differences between the two. First, in the broadcast the driver made reference to seeking aid from Joseph Gargan and Paul Markham. In the police report, no reference was made to them. Second, in the police statement, he said he went back to the party and had someone (unidentified) drive him back to Edgartown, while in his broadcast he refers to the aforesaid Gargan and Markham assisting him. These discrepancies do not alter the determination of the cause of death.

The next reference is that the police report and the broadcast are silent on many important details of the accident. While this is possibly so, proper subpoenaing of witnesses may or may not have substantiated this, but at the moment this court is not at liberty to speculate as to what those details might be.

Again, reference is made to witnesses who had knowledge of the accident and did not call the authorities. The court is unable to determine from the record who these witnesses were, to what they would testify, or why they were not subpoenaed.

One of the more substantial references in the petition was concerning the evidence of blood on the back of the deceased's blouse, as well as in her mouth and nose. Yet, the only positive testimony as to these was that this evidence was wholly consistent with death by drowning.

Equally significant was the testimony of Christopher Look, Jr. who testified as to the presence of the car of the driver near the bridge at about 12:40 a.m. on July 19, 1969 with a man and a woman in the front and a person or a sweater in the back, which left the scene hurriedly when his presence was evident and that this was the same car found in Poucha Pond that same day; also that he saw two unidentified girls and a man nearby. Again, this course of conduct by the driver does not suggest a cause of death other than as has been found.

With this in mind, let us examine the testimony in the petitioners' case that refutes their own contentions. In Chief Dominick Arena's police report, he states: "It was felt that because of the evidence at the scene, condition of the roadway and accident scene that there was no negligence on the part of the operator in the accident." The testimony of John N. Farrar, the scuba diver, is that at the scene there was nothing outstanding about the body other than that she was attractively dressed and fully clothed. That the submerged car had its ignition on, the car was in drive, the brake off, the light switch on, and it was full of gas. Also that the window on the driver's side was down and the door was locked. Dr. Donald Mills's testimony, reference to which will be made at length in the legal-medical portion of this opinion was that he found no signs of foul play or any criminal conduct. Finally, Eugene Frieh, the mortician, testified that in cleansing the body of Mary Jo Kopechne, he found no bruises, contusions or abrasions, except on a knuckle of her left hand.

In view of the above, it is difficult for this court to conclude that exhumation and autopsy are warranted. If there is testimony available to the petitioners that might establish the relief they seek, it has not been presented here.

Let us now address ourselves to the medical-legal aspect of this matter. As stated before, the petitioners must establish by a strong showing that the facts sought will be established by an exhumation and autopsy and there must be reasonable probability that a violation of the sepulchre will establish those facts.

In cases of death resulting from unnatural causes, autopsies before burial are performed as a matter of course. After interment, the legal test recited on pages four and five of this decision controls. As stated in this court's decision of October 9, 1969, " . . . It must not be overlooked that the Massachusetts authorities had the statutory right and opportunity to perform an autopsy prior to interment of the body of Mary Jo Kopechne, but once burial is complete, the aforementioned legal principles as to exhumation and autopsy must be considered."

Let us first review the medical testimony offered by the pathologists for the petitioners, that of Doctors Joseph W. Spellman, George G. Katsas, and Cyril H. Wecht. They all testified that if the body of Mary Jo Kopechne were exhumed and an autopsy performed, an interpretation of results would be more difficult but it would be entirely possible to make observations and draw valid conclusions. In the instance of Dr. Spellman, he testified he has performed autopsies on bodies interred for a period of five years. They also testified autopsies have frequently revealed causes of death not revealed by external examination, such as fractured skulls, hemorrhages within the brain, broken necks, broken ribs, ruptured internal organs and natural disease processes. In the case of Dr. Spellman, he testified that he attaches little significance to froth about the mouth or nose of a victim since it is found in other kinds of deaths such as heart failure, overdose of drugs, and death from respiratory depression. Dr. Katsas referred specifically to tests that might confirm death by drowning such as the presence of foreign material deep in the trachae or bronchi, hemorrhage in the middle ear and presence of diatoms and algae in the bones and remote areas of the body. However, on cross-examination, he testified that if all three tests proved negative, he would conclude that the cause of death was by drowning if he didn't find any other evidence of disease or injury in the remainder of the body. The only reference to reasonable medical certainty developed in the testimony of Dr. Wecht, who after reciting many general areas of causes of death, stated: "There would be an excellent opportunity to arrive at a quite substantial valid medical opinion that could be rendered by any competent pathologist with more than a reasonable degree of certainty." But of what? Even if we assume that an autopsy would reveal a broken neck or any other bone in the body, a fractured skull, the rupture of an internal organ, none of these would be incompatible with the manner in which the accident occurred. To consider any other cause of death at this time would give loose rein to speculation unsupported by any medical facts of record.

When we weigh this evidence with that of Dr. Donald Mills, who was also called on behalf of the petitioners, we immediately find an inconsistency within the petitioners' cause. Dr. Mills, after examination of the body of Mary Jo Kopechne, concluded and issued the death certificate with the cause of death as: "Asphyxiation by immersion - (Overturned submerged automobile)" i. e. death by drowning. His examination included a view of the body, finding a dead girl, well nourished, fully clothed, in total *rigor mortis.* He opened her blouse, put a stethoscope to her heart, percussed her chest with slight pressure and water came out of her nose and mouth. There was a fine white froth about her nose and mouth which was present before percussion. There were little cobwebs of blood on the foam which went directly to a little capillary area just on the left hand edge of her nostril. She obviously had much water in her respiratory tract since he applied pressure a number of times in varying degrees and each time water would well up and out. This pressure was on the chest, not the stomach. He saw no evidence of trauma of any kind after feeling her legs, arms, skull and back. That although he did not disrobe her, he did open her blouse and pulled her slacks down over her abdomen. To him, it was an "obvious case of drowning" since the foam about the nose and mouth, the cobwebs of blood from her nostril, the splashing sound of water in her chest and the emission of water from deep down are all common concomitants of drowning. It was his opinion that for all practical purposes his external examination excluded other causes of death. He also added that there was no evidence of foul play or any criminal conduct. To this we add the report of the blood test of the blood of the deceased which was negative as to barbituates and evidence of the consumption of only a small amount of alcoholic beverages.

While this may actually belong to the first category of consideration, the eliciting of truth in the promotion of justice, the fact is that after his examination Dr. Mills released the body to Mr. Frieh, the mortician, with a caveat that there should be no embalming until he cleared with the District Attorney's Office and the State Police. Only after it had been determined that there was no necessity for an autopsy did Dr. Mills then direct Mr. Frieh to embalm the body. This testimony of the delay in embalming was corroborated by Mr. Frieh, also a witness for petitioners.

Turning to the testimony of Dr. Werner Spitz, the pathologist testifying for the respondents, while his colleagues in his field did not attach particular significance to pinkish foam about the nose and mouth in drowning cases, he explained that when water enters the lungs under pressure, particularly salt water, there is a rupture of very small vessels and the blood from the rupture gives the foam a pinkish appearance. That when resuscitation stops, foam develops and being lighter than water, comes up. While there may be differences of opinion among pathologists, it would be illogical for this court not to accept that which is a logical explanation in view of all the attending circumstances. In addition, Dr. Spitz gave the only explanation as to the presence of blood on the back of the blouse of the deceased. He stated that when this pinkish foam begins to form, it runs down the face along the neck and makes a puddle behind the head and hence the blood on the back of the blouse. He said he couldn't imagine a drowning victim looking any different. He concedes that he would have liked to have had an autopsy when the body was first removed from the water, but that an exhumation and autopsy would be but of academic importance and added that, in his opinion, within medical certainty, Mary Jo Kopechne died from drowning.

The testimony of Dr. Henry C. Freimuth, a toxicologist, lends verity to the testimony of Drs. Mills and Spitz in that the stains on the blouse of the decedent were characteristic of the stains produced by pinkish foam from drowning victims.

In evaluating this medical testimony as it relates to the law of the Commonwealth of Pennsylvania, it must be concluded that the petitioners have failed to meet their burden of proof by a "strong showing that the facts sought will be established by an exhumation and autopsy" and that there is a "reasonable probability" that that which is sought warrants a violation of the sepulchre. *A fortiori*, from the testimony before this court, every reasonable probability leads to a conclusion that supports the original finding of the cause of death of Mary Jo Kopechne, asphyxiation by immersion, i. e. death by drowning.

In view of the testimony and law considered herein, and bearing in mind that courts are not reluctant to grant autopsies in given cases, we must be mindful that Joseph A. Kopechne and Gwen L. Kopechne, the parents of Mary Jo Kopechne, have indicated that they are unalterably opposed to exhumation and autopsy. Thus, it is incumbent that this court give weight to their objections. While their disapproval is not an absolute bar to an exhumation and autopsy, in view of the facts presented to this court, their objections are well taken.

It is the conclusion of this court that the facts presented herein are insufficient to support a finding of the cause of death of Mary Jo Kopechne other than asphyxiation by immersion.

Therefore, we enter the following:

ORDER

Now this 8th day of December, 1969, at 11:55 A.M., EST, it is hereby ordered and decreed that the objections of Joseph A. Kopechne and Gwen L. Kopechne, parents of Mary Jo Kopechne, are hereby sustained and the petitioners' request for exhumation and autopsy of the body of Mary Jo Kopechne is hereby denied.

BY THE COURT

_____

P.J.

Blythe H. Evans, Jr., Esq.,
Francis P. Burns, Esq.,

Edmund Dinis, Esq.,
Peter Gay, Esq.,
Armand Fernandes, Esq.,
Lance Garth, Esq.,

Joseph F. Flanagan, Esq.,
John E. O'Connor, Esq.,
Charles A. Shaffer, Esq.

THE NOQUEST INQUEST

THE DEATH of Mary Jo was a tragedy. The handling of the case by the Massachusetts Bench was an even greater tragedy. Senator Kennedy's guilty plea to leaving the scene of an accident, and the suspended sentence as per the agreement, satisfied neither the public nor the press. His television address when he was "free to tell" what had happened didn't tell anything and only increased the demand for the truth.

Weeks after the accident Edmund Dinis, District Attorney for the Southern District of Massachusetts, finally petitioned Judge Boyle for an inquest into the death. In retrospect it was a grandstand play. The only real efforts the authorities made were to help and protect the Senator.

Judge Boyle granted the request and set the proceedings for September 3, 1969, with the following stipulations:

> Only one witness at a time could appear in the court room; he could have counsel who would come and go with him and advise him of his constitutional rights;
>
> Any sequestering of witnesses would be decided by the judge;
>
> No listening devices or cameras would be allowed but counsel could arrange for stenographic transcripts;
>
> Courtroom seats were to be reserved exclusively for the press;
>
> The presence of Senator Kennedy would be required.

After these ground rules had been promulgated, Senator Kennedy's attorneys started up the merry-go-round by filing motions to have the inquest conducted similar to a criminal proceeding. They wanted all witnesses to have the right to examine and cross-examine witnesses and be able to produce witnesses of their own. They also wanted to have the right to refuse to testify. Above all, the attorneys wanted to keep the press out.

Judge Boyle denied the motions, so the Kennedy counsel appealed to the Massachusetts Supreme Court which stayed all proceedings until it could rule on the matter. Counsel for the Senator and the Senator were opposed to any inquest. If unavoidable, then it had to be secret. When this attitude resulted in unfavorable publicity they told the public this strategy had been decided upon by the Senator's lawyers. They floated the line that Senator Kennedy really opposed their decision and wanted everything out in the open but he had been overruled. But how can that be? Senator Kennedy was the client. He tells the lawyers how he wants his case handled. If the lawyers don't do what he says, he fires them. It is as simple as that; there is nothing complicated about it. Senator Kennedy is a lawyer, he knew all about this, but instead he sent up a smokescreen.

On October 30, 1969, the Massachusetts Supreme Court gave the Kennedy counsel and the Senator all they had asked for—plus a host of other goodies. The court really put it to the people of Massachusetts.

The court not only excluded the public *and the press* from the hearings, but it also excluded the hearings from the public and the press — perhaps forevermore. Cynics said the court jesters had taken over the bench.

The court ruled that records of the inquest proceedings would be locked away under the control of a superior court magistrate unless and until the Supreme Court certified that no prosecution was contemplated, that an indictment had been turned down, that the trial of the person for the death had been completed, or that a Superior Judge determined such a trial was not likely. In other words, the inquest record of proceedings was not to be used until it was no longer of any use. It was to be deep-sixed until all the troubled water had drained from under Dyke Bridge. One must admire, in the abstract, the sheer effrontery of the decision. Even chicanery is impressive when purveyed on such a grand scale.

With the Kennedy ground rules established, the inquest was duly held from January 5-8, 1970. The following witnesses appeared:

Edward M. Kennedy, U. S. Senator
Joseph F. Gargan
Paul H. Markham
John Crimmins
Raymond S. LaRosa
Charles C. Tretter
Maryellen Lyons
Esther Newberg
Rosemary Keough
Nance Lyons
Susan Tannenbaum
Police Chief Dominick J. Arena
John N. Farrar, Captain of the Edgartown Fire Department
Dr. Donald R. Mills, the County Assoc. Medical Examiner
Richard P. Hewitt, of the Chappaquiddick Island ferry
Russell E. Peachy, co-owner of the Shiretown Inn
Christopher S. Look, Jr., Deputy Sheriff
David R. Guay, an associate of Mr. Frieh
Eugene Frieh, Funeral Director
John J. O'Connor, telephone company official
Jared N. Grant, owner of the ferry
George W. Kennedy, a supervisor for the Reg. of Motor Vehicles
Dr. Robert D. Watt, trauma specialist-Cape Cod Medical Center
Dr. Milton F. Brougham, chief of neurosurgery at 4 hospitals
Eugene D. Jones, engineer
Donald L. Sullivan, employee of A.D. Little Inc.-road tests
John J. McHugh, State Police chemist
Dr. Robert W. Nevin, Dukes County Medical Examiner

Though the list of witnesses is impressive, the sum total is a mishmash of trivia and contradictions. The *Boston Globe* concluded: "Inept prosecution and preferential treatment of ... Kennedy by law enforcement and judicial officials probing the death of Mary Jo Kopechne apparently saved Sen. Kennedy from being charged with serious driving crimes, including manslaughter." Though it was rumored that Kennedy would try to stop the transcripts from being released before his 1970 election as Senator, they were made public when found to be quite harmless.

The inquest did not further the cause of justice. No unpleasantness marred the little tea party. There wasn't even any shadow-boxing. Everyone was on their good behavior and showed impeccably good manners. There were no surprises, no discoveries and no progress.

All those who had attended the "dull" party appeared in the role of witnesses and showed a marvelously cooperative spirit by agreeing with each other. You will be pleased to know they all had recovered their memories and agreed as to the time when the Senator and Mary Jo had left the party. Six months of counseling worked wonders. If Nixon had had such loyal followers, he might still be President.

Even all the attorneys conducted themselves properly throughout. There was no acrimony, or complaints and, of course, nothing of value was divulged. Judge Boyle did impute negligence to the Senator, but that fact has never been in doubt. Judge Boyle did *not,* repeat *not*—despite press reports to the contrary—recommend any prosecution of Senator Kennedy. The Judge was shrewdly able to play both ends of the stick. Senator Kennedy, in a Jovian decision, later rejected and overruled Judge Boyle's findings. The Senator said "the inference and ultimate findings of the judge's report are not justified and I reject them."

The inquest proceeding did serve to let Dr. Mills change his report on Mary Jo's death so that it would not reflect unfavorably upon the Senator. When he examined the body at the accident scene around 9:30 a.m., Dr. Mills said death had occurred from five to eight hours earlier—that is, between 1:30 and 4:30 a.m. This, coupled with the Senator's statement of going off the bridge a little after 11:15 p.m. put the Senator in a bad light. It meant that Mary Jo had stayed alive in the car at the bottom of Poucha Pond for at least two hours waiting to be saved by the Senator—who never even reported the accident.

It is assumed that this had been brought to the attention of the doctor by the time of the inquest. There he testified that the time of death had been six or more hours earlier—occurring from 3:30 a.m. on back, as needed, which constitutes a substantial re-estimate.

Judge Boyle must have been impressed to some degree by this testimony because he found that "death probably occurred between 11:30 p.m. on July 18, 1969, and 1:00 a.m. on July 19, 1969." That is, between eight and one-half and ten hours earlier than the 9:30 a.m. examination, as opposed to the original five to eight hours—up to a fifty percent difference.

If the doctor can make such a substantial change in his findings about the time of death without seeing any new evidence *of any kind,* why should we think he was any more careful in his findings as to the cause of death?

THE COMPLETE KENNEDY TESTIMONY

FROM THE HUNDREDS of pages of inquest transcripts, we present here the complete testimony of Senator Kennedy. While reading it through, keep in mind that Senator Kennedy laughed afterwards at the amount of trivia that he and his friends threw in. He later said: "I plan no further statement in this tragic matter. We must all live with the loss of Mary Jo and the pain that this has inflicted upon us." By such a gesture, Senator Kennedy allowed us all to share in the guilt.

THE COURT. Senator, would you take the witness stand?

SENATOR KENNEDY. Yes.
EDWARD M. KENNEDY, Sworn.

Examination by Mr. Dinis:

Q. Please give your name to the court.

A. Edward Moore Kennedy.

Q. And where is your legal residence, Mr. Kennedy?

A. 3 Charles River Square, Boston.

Q. Directing your attention to July 18, 1969, were there plans made by you to have a gathering on Martha's Vineyard Island?

A. There were.

Q. And what were these plans, Mr. Kennedy?

A. There were plans to participate in an annual sailing regatta in Edgartown on the dates of Friday, July 18th, and Saturday,

July 19th, and with my cousin Joe Gargan, Mr. Markham, Mr. LaRosa and a number of other people, a number of other individuals.

Q. When were these plans made?

A. Well, I had planned to participate in the regatta for some period of weeks.

Q. And were there any particular arrangements made for this gathering that we have just discussed?

A. Well, I had entered my boat in the regatta and had listed my crew. I had made those arrangements through my cousin, Joe Gargan.

Q. Were there any arrangements made to rent a house on Chappaquiddick?

A. I had made no such arrangements myself.

Q. Do you know who did?

A. Yes I do.

Q. May we have that name?

A. Mr. Gargan.

Q. Mr. Gargan. When did you arrive on the Island in conjunction with this gathering?

A. On July 18th, about 1 o'clock.

Q. 1:00 p.m.?

A. That is correct.

Q. Was there anyone with you?

A. No, I arrived by myself.

Q. And where did you stay, Senator?

A. Well, at the Shiretown Inn.

Q. Could you tell the court what your activities were during that afternoon from the time of your arrival?

A. Well, I arrived shortly after 1 o'clock on July 18th, was met by Mr. John B. Crimmins, driven through town, made a brief stop to pick up some fried clams, traveled by ferry to Chappaquiddick. Island to a small cottage there where I changed into a bathing suit, later visited the beach on I imagine the east side of that island for a brief swim, returned to the cottage and changed into another bathing suit, returned to the ferry slip and waded out to my boat, the VICTORIA, later participated in a race which ended approximately 6 o'clock.

Q. When did you check into the Shiretown Inn that day?

A. Sometime after 6:30, before 7 o'clock.

Q. Was anyone else in your party staying at the Shiretown Inn?

A. My cousin, Joe Gargan.

Q. Did your nephew, Joseph Kennedy, stay there?

A. Not to my knowledge.

Q. Now, following your checking in at the Shiretown Inn, what were your activities after that?

A. I returned to my room, visited with a few friends just prior to returning to that room on the porch which is outside the room of the Shiretown—outside my room at the Shiretown Inn, washed up briefly and returned to Chappaquiddick Island.

Q. What time did you return to Chappaquiddick Island at that time?

A. It was sometime shortly after 7 o'clock.

Q. And these friends that you had some conversation with at the Shiretown, do you have their names?

A. I do.

Q. May we have them?

A. Well, they are Mr. Ross Richards; I believe Mr. Stanley Moore was there that evening, and perhaps one or two of their crew, maybe Mrs. Richards. I am not familiar with the names. I know the other members of his crew, but I would say a group of approximately five or six.

Q. Do you recall the number of the room in which you were staying?

A. I believe it was 9. 7 or 9.

Q. Now, you say you returned to Chappaquiddick around 7:30 p.m.?

A. About 7:30.

Q. About that time. Now, you were familiar with the island of Chappaquiddick? Had you been there before?

A. Never been on Chappaquiddick Island before that day.

Q. And I believe you did state in one of your prepared statements that you had been visiting this island for about 30 years?

A. Martha's Vineyard Island.

Q. But you had never been to Chappaquiddick?

A. Never been to Chappaquiddick before 1:30 on the day of July 18th.

Q. Now, when you left the Shiretown Inn and returned to Chappaquiddick around 7:30 p.m., was there anyone with you?

A. Mr. Crimmins.

THE COURT. Might I just impose a moment and ask this question? You said you took a swim on Chappaquiddick Island

Friday afternoon?

THE WITNESS. That is correct.

THE COURT. Did you travel over Dyke Bridge to go to the beach on that swim?

THE WITNESS. Yes I did. If your Honor would permit me, at the time of the afternoon upon arrival on Chappaquiddick Island as at the time I was met at Martha's Vineyard Airport, I was driven by Mr. Crimmins to the cottage and to the beach, returned to the cottage subsequent to the point of rendezvous with the VICTORIA.

Q. What automobile was being used at that time?

A. A four-door Oldsmobile 88.

THE COURT. Might I ask you just a question? Who drove you. to the beach?

THE WITNESS. Mr. Crimmins

THE COURT. Was the car operated over the Dyke Bridge or was it left on the side?

THE WITNESS. No, it was operated over the Dyke Bridge.

Q. Was there anyone at the cottage when you arrived there at 7:30 p.m.?

A. No, I don't believe so.

Q. Had there been anyone there when you changed your swimming suits early in the afternoon?

A. Not when I first arrived there. Subsequently a group returned to the cottage after the swim.

Q. When you returned?

A. They were either outside the cottage or in its immediate vicinity. I wasn't aware whether they were inside the cottage or outside at the time I changed.

Q. Do you have the names of these persons who were there?

A. I can only give them in a general way because I am not absolutely sure which people were there at that particular time and which were in town making arrangements.

Q. Were a part of the group there later that evening?

A. Yes, they were.

Q. Were there any persons other than the crew that participated in the cook-out there?

A. No.

Q. Were there any other automobiles at that house on Chappaquiddick that afternoon?

A. Yes, there were.

Q. Do you know how many?

A. Just two to my best knowledge. One other vehicle, so there were two in total to my best knowledge.

Q. Did you have any plans at that time to stay on Chappaquiddick Island?

A. No, I did not.

Q. Did you plan on staying overnight?

A. No, I did not.

Q. And how long did you actually stay on Chappaquiddick Island that evening?

A. Well, to my best knowledge I would say 1:30 in the morning on July 19th.

THE COURT. When you left?

THE WITNESS. When I left.

THE COURT. When you left.

Q. What transpired after you arrived at the cottage after your arrival at 7:30 p.m.?

A. Well, after my arrival I took a bath in the tub that was available at the cottage, which was not available at the Shiretown Inn, and soaked my back. I later was joined by Mr. Markham who arrived some time about 8 o'clock, engaged in conversations with Mr. Markham until about 8:30, and the rest of the group arrived at 8:30 or shortly thereafter. During this period of time Mr. Crimmins made me a drink of rum and Coca-Cola.

Q. Now, did you have dinner at the cottage?

A. Well, at 8:30 the rest of the group arrived and were made to feel relaxed and at home, enjoyed some hors d'oeuvres, were served a drink, those who wanted them, and steaks were cooked on an outdoor burner by Mr. Gargan at about approximately quarter of 10, I would think.

Q. Do you recall who did the cooking? Was there any cooking at that time?

A. Yes, there was.

Q. And do you recall who performed the job?

A. Well, principally Mr. Gargan. I think the young ladies did some of the cooking of the hors d'oeuvres and some of the gentlemen helped in starting the charcoal fire, and also the cooking of the steaks, the making of the salad and so forth.

Q. Were there any drinks served, cocktails served?

A. There were.

Q. Did anyone in particular tend bar or have charge of this particular responsibility?

A. Well, I tried initially to respond to any of the requests of the guests when they arrived and then I think most of the individuals made their drinks after that, what they wanted.

Q. And I believe you said earlier that Mr. Gargan was in charge of the arrangements of renting the cottage and making the preparation for the cookout, as far as you know?

A. That is correct. I would say the other gentlemen did some of the purchasing of the food and others got the stuff for the cookout. Others—some brought the steaks—others brought the other ingredients for the cookout.

Q. Did you have occasion to leave the cottage at any time during the evening?

A. That is correct.

Q. Did you leave more than once?

A. That is correct.

Q. Well, will you please give us the sequence of events with regard to your activities after 8:30 p.m.?

A. Well, during the course of the evening, as I mentioned, I engaged in conversation and recollections with those that were attending this group which were old friends of myself and our families. Some alcoholic beverages were served.

THE COURT. Excuse me. Read the question back to me.

(Question read.)

Q. How many times did you leave the cottage that evening, Senator?

A. Two different occasions.

Q. Would you please tell us about the first time?

A. The first time I left at approximately 11:15 the evening of July 18 and I left a second time, sometime after midnight, by my best judgement, it would be approximately 12:15 for the second time. On the second occasion I never left the cottage itself, I left the immediate vicinity of the cottage which was probably 15 or 20 feet outside the front door.

Q. And when you left the second time, did you then return to Edgartown?

A. Sometime after I left the second time, I returned to Edgartown. I did not return immediately to Edgartown.

Q. Now, when you left on the first occasion, were you alone?

A. I was not alone.

Q. And who was with you?

A. Miss Mary Jo Kopechne was with me.

Q. Anyone else?

A. No.

Q. And did you use the 88 Oldsmobile that was later taken from the river?

A. I used—yes, I did.

Q. What time did Miss Kopechne arrive at the cottage that evening?

A. My best knowledge approximately 8:30.

Q. At 8:30 p.m.?

A. That is correct.

Q. Do you know how she arrived?

A. To my best knowledge she arrived in a white Valiant that brought some of the people to that party.

Q. Do you know who owned that car?

A. I believe it was a rented car.

Q. Do you know who rented it?

A. No. One of the group that was there, I would say. I'm not sure.

Q. When you left the party at 11:15 with Miss Kopechne, had you had any prior conversation with her?

A. Yes, I had.

Q. Will you please give that conversation to the court?

A. At 11:15 I was talking with Miss Kopechne perhaps for some minutes before that period of time. I noticed the time, desired to leave and return to the Shiretown Inn and indicated to her that I was leaving and returning to town. She indicated to me that she was desirous of leaving, if I would be kind enough to drop her back at her hotel. I said, well, I'm leaving immediately; spoke with Mr. Crimmins, requested the keys for the car and left at that time.

Q. Does Mr. Crimmins usually drive your car or drive you?

A. On practically every occasion.

Q. On practically every occasion?

A. Yes.

Q. Was there anything in particular that changed those circumstances at this particular time?

A. Only to the extent that Mr. Crimmins, as well as some of the other fellows that were attending the cookout, were concluding their meal, enjoying the fellowship, and it didn't appear to me to be necessary to require him to bring me back to Edgartown.

Q. Do you know whether or not Miss Kopechne had her pocketbook with her at the time you left?

A. I do not.

Q. Mr. Kennedy, how were you dressed at the time you left the first time at 11:15?

A. In a pair of light slacks and a dark jersey and I believe shoes, moccasins, and a back brace.

Q. Do you know how Miss Kopechne was dressed, do you recall that?

A. Only from what I have read in the—I understand, slacks and a blouse, sandals, perhaps a sweater; I'm not completely——

Q. And when you left the house at Chappaquiddick at 11:15, you were driving?

A. That is correct.

Q. And where was Miss Kopechne seated?

A. In the front seat.

Q. Was there any other person—was there any other person in the car at that time?

A. No.

Q. Was there any other item, thing or object in the car at that time of any size?

A. Well, not to my knowledge at that particular time. I have read subsequently in newspapers that there was another person in that car, but that is only what I have read about and to my knowledge at that time there wasn't any other object that I was aware of.

Q. Well, Senator, was there any other person in the car?

A. No, there was not.

Q. And on leaving the cottage, Senator—Mr. Kennedy, where did you go?

A. Well, I traveled down, I believe it is Main Street, took a right on Dyke Road and drove off the bridge at Dyke Bridge.

Q. Did you at any time drive into Cemetery Road?

A. At no time did I drive into Cemetery Road.

Q. Did you back that car up at any time?

A. At no time did I back that car up.

Q. Did you see anyone on the road between the cottage and the bridge that night?

A. I saw no one on the road between the cottage and the bridge.

THE COURT: Did you stop the car at any time?

THE WITNESS: I did not stop the car at any time.

Q. (By Mr. Dinis) Did you pass any other vehicle at that time?

A. I passed no other vehicle at that time. I passed no other vehicle and I saw no other person and I did not stop the car at any time between the time I left the cottage and went off the bridge.

Q. Now, would you describe your automobile to the Court?

A. Well, it is a four-door black sedan, Oldsmobile.

Q. Do you recall the registration plate?

A. I do not recall the registration plate.

Q. Senator, I show you a photograph and ask you whether or not you can identify that?

A. I believe that to be my car.

Q. Your automobile?

A. Yes.

MR. DINIS: This is the automobile that the Senator identifies as his.

THE COURT: I think we ought to have a little more. This location is—

THE WITNESS: I have no—

THE COURT: Mr. Kennedy says this is his automobile after the accident and he doesn't know the location of where the automobile is or when this picture was taken. Mark that Exhibit 1.

(The picture was marked Exhibit No. 1.)

Q. (By Mr. Dinis) I show you two photographs. Are you able to identify the automobile in the photographs?

A. In my best knowledge that is my automobile that went off the bridge.

Q. In examining the registration, would that help you at all?

A. I believe that is my vehicle.

MR. DINIS: If your Honor pleases, these are photographs that have been taken of the car which has been removed from the water.

THE COURT: Well, are you going to have any witness testify when these were taken?

MR. DINIS: Yes, your Honor, we can have that.

THE COURT: And where they were taken?

MR. DINIS: Yes, your Honor.

THE COURT: You identify the car as being your car?

THE WITNESS: I do, your Honor, it is my best judgement that it is my car. I don't think there is really much question.

THE COURT: I would prefer that you wait until you put on the witness that is going to say—

MR. DINIS: May it be allowed de bene, your Honor? The sequence in presenting this evidence is for the purpose of — we couldn't — all I want to establish is that the Senator says they look like his car and then we will later have testimony as to where they were taken.

THE COURT: Well, I would rather not get into the trial technique.

MR. DINIS: I appreciate that.

THE COURT: De bene. I prefer you wait until you have the witness to identify it. I want to avoid as much as possible, Mr. Dinis, any trial technique.

THE WITNESS: I would just say to the best knowledge that those are pictures of my car that were shown to me.

Q. (By Mr. Dinis) In your conversation with Miss Kopechne prior to your leaving at 11:15, did she indicate to you any necessity for returning to Martha's Vineyard or to Edgartown?

A. Prior to that conversation, no.

Q. Well, when she left with you, where was she going?

A. Back to her hotel.

Q. Now, when you left at 11:15 do you know how many persons remained at the house on Chappaquiddick?

A. To my best judgement most of them were in the cottage when I left. I didn't make a count of who was there, but I think most of them were there.

THE COURT: Well, do you know of anyone having left before?

THE WITNESS: No, I don't except on one occasion where—

THE COURT: No, I mean having left permanently.

THE WITNESS: No, no.

Q. (By Mr. Dinis) Did anyone else have access to your automobile that afternoon or that evening?

A. Oh, yes.

Q. And who might that have been?

A. Well, Mr. Crimmins certainly had access that afternoon and I believe Mr. Tretter borrowed the car to return to Edgartown briefly. I couldn't say of my own knowledge that he used that car rather than the Valiant, but he may very well have, and I would say during the course of the afternoon it was generally available to any of the group to use for transportation.

Q. Do you recall how fast you were driving when you made the right on Dyke Road?

A. No, I would say approximately seven or eight miles an hour.

Q. And what were the lighting conditions and weather conditions that evening?

A. Well, as you know, there are no lights on that road. The road was dry. There was a reasonable amount of humidity. The night was clear, extremely dark.

Q. Were the windows of the automobile open or closed?

A. Some of the windows were open and some were closed.

Q. Do you have an air-conditioner in that car?

A. No, I don't.

THE COURT: Could we know which were opened and which were closed?

THE WITNESS: I read, your Honor—

THE COURT: No, no, of your own knowledge.

THE WITNESS: Of my own knowledge?

THE COURT: What about the window on your side?

THE WITNESS: I would expect it was open.

THE COURT: You don't remember that?

THE WITNESS: I don't remember that.

THE COURT: How about the windows on the passenger's side?

THE WITNESS: I really don't remember.

THE COURT: Was it a warm night?

THE WITNESS: I would think it was cool at that hour, but I really have no personal knowledge as to which windows were open or closed. I have read subsequently which ones were open or blown open, but at that time I really don't recall.

Q. (By Mr. Dinis) Well, Mr. Kennedy, was the window on the driver's side open?

A. Yes, it was.

Q. Do you recall whether or not the window in the car seat behind the driver was open?

A. I don't recall.

Q. And you have no recollection as to the windows on the passenger's side of the vehicle?

A. No, I really don't.

Q. How fast were you driving on Dyke Road?

A. Approximately 20 miles an hour.

Q. Were the brakes of your Oldsmobile in order at that time?

A. I believe so. There is no reason to assume otherwise. Mr. Crimmins takes very good care of the car.

Q. Well, were you aware at the time that you were driving on a dirt road when you hit, when you turned onto Dyke Road?

A. Well, sometime during the drive down Dyke Road I was aware that I was on an unpaved road, yes.

Q. At what point, Mr. Kennedy, did you realize that you were driving on a dirt road?

A. Just sometime when I was—I don't remember any specific time when I knew I was driving on an unpaved road. I was generally aware sometime going down that road that it was unpaved, like many of the other roads here in Martha's Vineyard and Nantucket and Cape Cod.

Q. When you left the house at 11:15, what was your destination?

A. The Katama Shores, the ferry slip, the Katama Shores, Shiretown.

Q. Now, had you been over that road from the ferry slip to the cottage more than once that day?

A. Yes, I had.

Q. Did you recall at the time that you noticed you were driving on a dirt road, that road from the ferry slip to the house had been paved?

A. Well, Mr. Dinis, I would say that I, having lived on Cape Cod and having visited these islands, I am aware some roads are paved.

THE COURT: I am sorry, that is not quite responsive. The question is whether or not you realized the road from the ferry slip to the cottage was paved.

MR. DINIS: That is correct.

THE WITNESS: Yes.

THE COURT: That is, did you become aware of it during your trips?

THE WITNESS: Well, I would just say it was not of particular notice to me whether it was paved or unpaved.

THE COURT: Were you driving the car either one of those times?

THE WITNESS: I was not.

Q. (By Mr. Dinis) Well, while you were driving down Dyke Road and after you noticed it was a dirt road and you were driving at 20 miles an hour, what happened, Mr. Kennedy?

A. Well, I became —

THE COURT: I'm going to ask one question. At any time after you got on the unpaved road, the so-called Dyke Road, did you have a realization that you were on the wrong road?

THE WITNESS: No.

THE COURT: Do you remember the question?

THE WITNESS: After I realized it was an unpaved road, what did I become aware of?

Q. (By Mr. Dinis) Well, after you realized it was an unpaved road, and that you were driving at 20 miles an hour, what happened then?

A. I went off Dyke Bridge or I went off a bridge.

Q. You went off a bridge into the water?

A. That is correct.

Q. Did you apply the brakes of that automobile prior to going off into the water?

A. Perhaps a fraction of a second before.

Q. What prompted you to do that?

A. Well, I was about to go off a bridge and I applied the brakes.

Q. Were there any lights in that area?

A. Absolutely no lights in that area I noticed other than the lights on my vehicle.

Q. Did you realize at that moment that you were not heading for the ferry?

A. At the moment I went off the bridge, I certainly did.

Q. Do you recall whether or not the — strike that question — well, what happened after that, Senator?

A. Well, I remembered the vehicle itself just beginning to go off the Dyke Bridge and the next thing I recall is the movement of Mary Jo next to me, the struggling, perhaps hitting or kicking me and I, at this time, opened my eyes and realized I was upsidedown, that water was crashing in on me, that it was pitch black. I knew that and I was able to get a half a gulp, I would say, of air before I became completely immersed in the water. I realized that Mary Jo and I had to get out of the car.

I can remember reaching down to try to get the doorknob of the car and lifting the door handle and pressing against the door and it was not moving. I can remember reaching what I thought was down, which was really up, to where I thought the window was and feeling along the side to see if the window was open and the window was closed, and I can remember the last sensation of being completely out of air and inhaling a lung full of water and assuming that I was going to drown and the full realization that no one was going to be looking for us that night until the next morning and that I wasn't going to get out of that car alive and then somehow I can remember coming up to the last energy of just pushing, pressing, and coming up to the surface.

Q. Senator, how did you realize that you were upside down in the car?

A. Because — that was a feeling that I had as soon as I became aware that — the water rushing in and the blackness, I knew that I was upside down. I really wasn't sure of anything, but I thought I was upside down.

Q. Were you aware that the windows on the passenger's side were blown out of the car, were smashed?

A. I have read that subsequently. I wasn't aware of it at the time.

Q. Were you aware that there was any water rushing in on the passenger's side?

A. There was complete blackness. Water seemed to rush in from every point, from the windshield, from underneath me, above me. It almost seemed like you couldn't hold the water back even with your hands. What I was conscious of was the rushing of the water, the blackness, the fact that it was impossible to even hold it back.

Q. And you say at that time you had a thought to the effect that you may not be found until morning?

A. I was sure that I was going to drown.

Q. Did you make any observations of the condition of Miss Kopechne at that time?

A. At what time?

Q. At that particular moment when you were thrashing around in the car?

A. Well, at the moment I was thrashing around I was trying to find a way that we both could get out of the car, and at some time after I tried the door and the window I became convinced I was never going to get out.

Q. Was the window closed at that time?

A. The window was open.

Q. On the driver's side?

A. That's correct.

Q. And did you go through the window to get out of the car?

A. I have no idea in the world how I got out of that car.

Q. Do you have any recollection as to how the automobile left the bridge and went over into the water?

A. How it left the bridge?

Q. Yes. What particular path did it take.

A. No.

Q. Did it turn over?

A. I have no idea.

THE COURT: I would like to inquire, Mr. Dinis, something about the operation of the car, if you are finished.

MR. DINIS: Go right ahead, your Honor.

THE COURT: You are driving along the dike sandy road and you are approaching the Dyke Bridge. Now, you can describe to me what you saw, what you did, what happened from the point when you first saw the bridge?

THE WITNESS: I would estimate the time to be a fraction of a second from the time that I first saw the bridge and was on the bridge.

THE COURT: Did you have on your high beams, do you remember?

THE WITNESS: I can't remember.

THE COURT: It is your custom to use high beams when you are driving?

THE WITNESS: I rarely drive. I really couldn't tell you. I may have.

THE COURT: It is recommended.

THE WITNESS: It is recommended, but sometimes if there is a mist you see better with low beams.

THE COURT: Did you see the bridge before you actually reached it?

THE WITNESS: The split second before I was on it.

THE COURT: Did you see that it was at an angle to the road?

THE WITNESS: The bridge was at an angle to the road?

THE COURT: Yes.

THE WITNESS: Just before going on it I saw that.

THE COURT: Did you make any attempt to turn your wheels to follow that angle?

THE WITNESS: I believe I did, your Honor. I would assume that I did try to go on the bridge. It appeared to me at that time that the road went straight.

THE COURT: Were you looking ahead at the time you were driving the car, at that time?

THE WITNESS: Yes, I was.

THE COURT: Your attention was not diverted by anything else?

THE WITNESS: No, it wasn't.

THE COURT: I don't want to foreclose you, Mr. Dinis, I want to go into the question of alcoholic beverages. Perhaps you had that in mind later?

MR. DINIS: Yes, your Honor.

THE COURT: All right.

Q. Going back to the cottage earlier in the day, you stated, you volunteered the information that you had a rum and Coca-Cola?

A. That is right.

Q. Did you have more than one?

A. Yes, I did.

Q. How many did you have?

A. I had two.

THE COURT: What time was this?

THE WITNESS: The first was about 8 o'clock.

THE COURT: I would like to go back before that. I think you said you visited some friends at the Shiretown Inn?

THE WITNESS: That is right.

THE COURT: Did you do some drinking then?

THE WITNESS: I had about a third of a beer at that time.

THE COURT: And you had nothing further until this?

THE WITNESS: No, I had nothing further.

Q. And when did you have the second rum and coke?

A. The second some time later on in the evening. I think before dinner, sometime about 9:15. It would be difficult for me to say.

Q. Now, during the afternoon of the 18th did you have occasion to spend some time with your nephew, Joseph Kennedy?

A. I might have greeted him in a brief greeting, but otherwise, no. I knew he was concerned about where he was going to stay; that he had some reservations and that somehow they had gotten cancelled, but I would say other than a casual passing and a greeting, I would say no.

Q. He was at this time on Chappaquiddick Island?

A. Not to my knowledge. I never saw him at Chappaquiddick.

Q. Did you see him at the Shiretown Inn?

A. I might have seen him in inquiring whether he could stay at the Shiretown Inn.

Q. Did he stay with you in your room?

A. No, he did not.

THE COURT: I would like to ask some questions. You said you had a portion of beer late in the afternoon at the Shiretown Inn?

THE WITNESS: That is correct.

THE COURT: Then you had two rums and coke at this cottage at Chappaquiddick Island sometime after you arrived at about 8:30?

THE WITNESS: That is right.

THE COURT: Who poured those drinks?

THE WITNESS: Mr. Crimmins poured the first one. I poured the second one.

THE COURT: What amount of rum did you put in?

THE WITNESS: It would be difficult, your Honor, to estimate.

THE COURT: Well, by ounces.

THE WITNESS: By ounces? I suppose two ounces.

THE COURT: I mean, some people pour heavy drinks. Some pour light drinks.

THE WITNESS: Yes.

THE COURT: When did you take the last one?

THE WITNESS: I would think about 9 o'clock. The only way I could judge that, your Honor, would be that I ate about 10 and it was sometime before I ate.

THE COURT: You had nothing alcoholic to drink after eating?

THE WITNESS: No, I didn't.

THE COURT: How much liquor was at this cottage?

THE WITNESS: There were several bottles so that I wouldn't be able to tell specifically.

THE COURT: Not a large supply?

THE WITNESS: I wouldn't be able to tell how much. There was an adequate supply.

THE COURT: Was there a sustained amount of drinking by the group?

THE WITNESS: No, there wasn't.

THE COURT: By any particular person?

THE WITNESS: Not that I noticed. There wasn't prior to the time I left.

THE COURT: Mr. Hanify, you have advised your client of his constitutional rights?

MR. HANIFY: Yes, I have, your Honor.

THE COURT: Were you at any time that evening under the influence of alcohol?

THE WITNESS: Absolutely not.

THE COURT: Did you imbibe in any narcotic drugs that evening?

THE WITNESS: Absolutely not.

THE COURT: Did anyone at the party to your knowledge?

THE WITNESS: No, absolutely not.

THE COURT: In your opinion were you sober at the time that you operated the motor vehicle to the Dyke Bridge?

THE WITNESS: Absolutely sober.

Q. Senator Kennedy, what did you do immediately following your release from the automobile?

A. I was swept away by the tide that was flowing at an extraordinary rate through that narrow cut there and was swept along by the tide and called Mary Jo's name until I was able to make my way to what would be the east side of that cut, waded up to about my waist and started back to the car, at this time I was gasping and belching and coughing, I went back just in front of the car.

Now the headlights of that car were still on and I was able to get what I thought was the front of the car, although it was difficult — and I was able to identify the front of the car from the rear of the car by the lights themselves. Otherwise I don't think I would be able to tell.

Q. How far were you swept along by the current?

A. Approximately 30 to 40 feet.

Q. Did you pass under the bridge?

A. The vehicle went over the bridge on the south side and rested on the south side, and that was the direction the water was flowing, and I was swept I would think to the south or probably east, which would be the eastern shore.

Q. Some 30 feet?

A. I would think 30 to 40 feet.

Q. Now, in order to get back to the car was it necessary for you to swim?

A. I couldn't swim at that time because of the current. I waded into—swam to where I could wade and then waded along the shore up to where I could go to the front of the car and start diving in an attempt to rescue Mary Jo.

Q. Was the front of the car facing a westerly direction?

A. I would think it was facing in a northerly direction.

Q. Well, in regard to the bridge could you describe the location of the automobile with relation to the bridge?

A. Well, your Honor, in the direction of north and south. I will do the best I can.

THE COURT: We don't have any map, do we?

MR. TELLER: The bridge runs north and south, fairly close to north and south.

THE COURT: That is coming towards Edgartown would be north and towards the ocean would be south?

MR. TELLER: Yes, sir.

MR. DINIS: May we use the chalk, your Honor?

THE COURT: Yes, if it is helpful.

Q. Would that be helpful, Mr. Kennedy?

A. It may be.

Q. I believe there is a board behind you. Assuming the bridge is north and south—

A. Yes.

(Witness draws sketch on blackboard.)

I would bet that the bridge runs more east-west than north-south.

MR. TELLER: Not directly north, but southeast-northwest.

Q. Will you indicate, Mr. Kennedy, Edgartown?

A. I would rather have counsel draw and respond. I will be delighted to do whatever the court desires.

THE COURT: It is only for the purposes of illustration.

THE WITNESS: I suppose the road runs something like this.

THE COURT: You are trying to get the relation of the car to the bridge?

MR. DINIS: Yes, your Honor.

Q. As you went off the bridge?

A. I think it was like this.

THE COURT: All right, Mr. Dinis.

Q. Mr. Kennedy, after you emerged from the automobile you say you were swept some 30 feet away from the car, is that correct?

A. In this direction (indicating).

Q. And how much time did it take you after you left the automobile to be swept down to about 30 feet, down the river?

A. By the time I came up I was, the best estimate would be somewhere over here, which would be probably 8-10 feet, it is difficult for me to estimate specifically, and I think by the time I was able at least to regain my strength, I would say it is about 30 feet after which time I swam in this direction until I was able to wade, and wade back up here to this point here, and went over to the front of the car, where the front of the car was, and crawled over to here, dove here, and the tide would sweep out this way there, and then I dove repeatedly from this side until, I would say, the end, and then I was swept away the first couple of times, again back over to this side, I would come back again and again to this point here, or try perhaps the third or fourth time to gain entrance to some area here until at the very end when I couldn't hold my breath any longer. I was breathing so heavily it was down to just a matter of seconds. I would hold my breath and I could barely get underneath the water. I was just able to hold on to the metal undercarriage here, and the water itself came right out to where I was breathing, and I could hold on, I knew that I just could not get under water any more.

Q. And you were fully aware at that time of what was transpiring?

A. Well, I was fully aware that I was trying to get the girl out of that car and I was fully aware that I was doing everything I possibly could to get her out of the car and I was fully aware at that time that my head was throbbing and my neck was aching and I was breathless, and at that time, the last time, hopelessly exhausted.

Q. You were not confused at that time?

A. Well, I knew that there was a girl in that car and I had to get her out. I knew that.

Q. And you took steps to get her out?

A. I tried the best I thought I possibly could to get her out.

Q. But there was no confusion in your mind about the fact that there was a person in the car and that you were doing the best you could to get that person out?

A. I was doing the very best I could to get her out.

THE COURT: May I ask you some questions about the depth of the water?

THE WITNESS: Yes.

THE COURT: You were not able to stand up at any point around any portion of that car?

THE WITNESS: No, it was not possible to stand. The highest level of the car to the surface were the wheels and the undercarriage itself. When I held on to the undercarriage and the tide would take me down, it was up to this point. (Indicating)

Q. Mr. Kennedy, how many times if you recall did you make an effort to submerge and get into the car?

A. I would say seven or eight times. At the last point, the seventh or eighth attempts were barely more than five or eight second submersions below the surface. I just couldn't hold my breath any longer. I didn't have the strength even to come down even close to the window or the door.

Q. And do you know how much time was used in these efforts?

A. It would be difficult for me to estimate, but I would think probably 15-20 minutes.

Q. And did you then remove yourself from the water?

A. I did.

Q. And how did you do that?

A. Well, in the last dive, I lost contact with the vehicle again and I started to come down this way here and I let myself float and came over to this shore and I came onto this shore here, and I sort of crawled and staggered up some place in here and was very exhausted and spent on the grass.

Q. On the west bank of the river?

A. Yes.

Q. As indicated by that chart?

A. Yes, that's correct.

Q. And how long did you spend resting?

A. Well, I would estimate probably 15-20 minutes trying to get my—I was coughing up the water and I was exhausted and I suppose the best estimate would be 15 or 20 minutes.

Q. Now, did you say earlier you spent 15-20 minutes trying to recover Miss Kopechne?

A. That is correct.

Q. And you spent another 15 or 20 minutes recovering on the west side of the river?

A. That is correct.

Q. Now, following your rest period, Senator, what did you do after that?

A. Well, I—

Q. You may remain seated.

A. All right, after I was able to regain my breath, I went back to the road and I started down the road and it was extremely dark and I could make out no forms or shapes or figures, and the only way that I could even see the path of the road was looking down the silhouettes of the trees on the two sides and I could watch the silhouette of the trees on the two sides and I started going down that road, walking, trotting, jogging, stumbling as fast as I possibly could.

Q. Did you pass any houses with lights on?

A. Not to my knowledge; never saw a cottage with a light on.

Q. And did you then return to the cottage where your friends had been gathered?

A. That is correct.

Q. And how long did that take you to make that walk, do you recall?

A. I would say approximately 15 minutes.

Q. And then you arrived at the cottage, as you did, is that true?

A. That is true.

Q. Did you speak to anyone there?

A. Yes, I did.

Q. And with whom did you speak?

A. Mr. Ray LaRosa.

Q. And what did you tell him?

A. I said, get me Joe Gargan.

Q. And was Joe Gargan there?

A. He was there.

Q. He was at the party?

A. Yes.

THE COURT: Excuse me a moment. Did you go inside the cottage?

THE WITNESS: No, I didn't go inside.

Q. (By Mr. Dinis) What did you do? Did you sit in the automobile at that time?

A. Well, I came up to the cottage, there was a car parked there, a white vehicle, and as I came up to the back of the vehicle, I saw Ray LaRosa at the door and I said Ray get me Joe, and he mentioned something like right away, and as he was going in to get Joe, I got in the back of the car.

Q. In this white car?

A. Yes.

Q. And now, did Joe come to you?

A. Yes, he did.

Q. And did you have conversation with him?

A. Yes I did.

Q. Would you tell us what the conversation was?

A. I said, you had better get Paul, too.

Q. Did you tell him what happened?

A. At that time I said, better get Paul, too.

Q. What happened after that?

A. Well, Paul came out, got in the car. I said, there has been a terrible accident, we have got to go, and we took off down the road, the main road there.

Q. How long had you known Mr. LaRosa prior to this evening?

A. Eight years, ten years, eight or ten years.

Q. Were you familiar with the fact or—strike that—did you have any knowledge that Mr. LaRosa had some experience in skindiving?

A. No, I never did.

Q. Now, before you drove down the road, did you make any further explanations to Mr. Gargan or Mr. Markham?

A. Before driving? No, sir. I said, there has been a terrible accident, let's go, and we took off—

Q. And they went—

A. Driving.

Q. And they drove hurriedly down?

A. That is right.

Q. And where did you stop the white automobile that you were riding in?

A. Mr. Gargan drove the vehicle across the bridge to some location here (indicating) and turned it so that its headlights shown over the water and over the submerged vehicle. (Indicating on blackboard.)

Q. And what happened after the three of you arrived there?

A. Mr. Gargan and Mr. Markham took off all their clothes, dove into the water, and proceeded to dive repeatedly to try and save Mary Jo.

Q. Now, do you recall what particular time this is now when the three of you were at the—

A. I think it was 12:20, Mr. Dinis. I believe that I looked at the Valiant's clock and believe that it was 12:20.

Q. Now, Mr. LaRosa remained at the cottage?

A. Yes, he did.

Q. Was Mr. LaRosa aware of the accident?

A. No, he hadn't heard—no, I don't believe so.

Q. No one else at the cottage was told of the accident?

A. No.

Q. How many times did you go back to Dyke Bridge that night?

A. Well, that was the only—

Q. After the accident, that was the only occasion?

A. The only time, the only occasion.

Q. Now, how long did Mr. Markham and Mr. Gargan remain there with you on that particular occasion?

A. I would think about 45 minutes.

Q. And they were unsuccessful in entering the car?

A. Well, Mr. Gargan got halfway in the car. When he came out he was scraped all the way from his elbow, underneath his arm was all bruised and bloodied, and this is the one time that he was able to gain entrance I believe into the car itself.

Q. And did he talk to you about his experience in trying to get into the car?

A. Well, I was unable to, being exhausted, to get into the water, but I could see exactly what was happening and made some suggestions.

Q. So that you were participating in the rescue efforts?

A. Well, to that extent.

Q. You were fully aware of what was transpiring at that time?

A. Well, I was fully aware that Joe Gargan and Paul Markham were trying to get in that car and rescue that girl, I certainly would say that.

Q. Did you know at that time or did you have any idea how long Mary Jo had been in the water?

A. Well, I knew that some time had passed.

Q. Well, you testified earlier that you spent some 15 or 20 minutes of—

A. Well, Mr. District Attorney, I didn't add up the time that I was adding to rescue her and time on the beach, the shore, and the time to get back and the time it took back and calculate it.

Q. Was it fair to say that she was in the water about an hour?

A. Yes, it is.

Q. Was there any effort made to call for assistance?

A. No, other than the assistance of Mr. Gargan and Mr. Markham.

Q. I know, but they failed in their efforts to recover—

A. That is right.

Q. Miss Kopechne?

A. That is correct.

MR. DINIS: I believe, your Honor, before the witness left the courtroom the question was whether or not any assistance had been asked for.

THE COURT: I think the answer had been no.

Q. (By Mr. Dinis) And now may I ask you, Mr. Kennedy, was there any reason why no additional assistance was asked for?

A. Was there any reason?

Q. Yes, was there any particular reason why you did not call either the police or the fire department?

A. Well, I intended to report it to the police.

THE COURT: That is not quite responsive to the question.

Q. Was there any reason why it did not happen at that time?

THE COURT: Call for assistance.

THE WITNESS: I intended to call for assistance and to report the accident to the police within a few short moments after going back into the car.

Q. I see, and did something transpire to prevent this?

A. Yes.

Q. What was that?

A. With the Court's indulgence, to prevent this, if the Court would permit me I would like to be able to relate to the Court the immediate period following the time that Mr. Gargan, Markham and I got back in the car.

THE COURT: I have no objection.

MR. DINIS: I have no objection.

THE WITNESS: Responding to the question of the District Attorney—

MR. DINIS: Yes.

THE WITNESS: —at some time, I believe it was about 45 minutes after Gargan and Markham dove they likewise became exhausted and no further diving efforts appeared to be of any avail and they so indicated to me and I agreed. So they came out of the water and came back into the car and said to me, Mr. Markham and Mr. Gargan at different times as we drove down the road towards the ferry that it was necessary to report this accident. A lot of different thoughts came into my mind at that time about how I was going to really be able to call Mrs. Kopechne at some time in the middle of the night to tell her that her daughter was drowned, to be able to call my own mother and my own father, relate to them, my wife, and I even—even though I knew that Mary Jo Kopechne was dead and believed firmly that she was in the back of that car, I willed that she remained alive.

As we drove down that road I was almost looking out the front window and windows trying to see her walking down that road. I related this to Gargan and Markham and they said they understood this feeling, but it was necessary to report it. And about this time we came to the ferry crossing and I got out of the car and we talked there just a few minutes.

I just wondered how all of this could possibly have happened. I also had sort of a thought and the wish and desire and the hope that suddenly this whole accident would disappear, and they reiterated that this has to be reported and I understood at the time I left that ferry boat, left the slip where the ferry boat was, that it had to be reported and I had full intention of reporting it, and I mentioned to Gargan and Markham something like, "You take care of the girls, I will take care of the accident,"— that is what I said and I dove into the water.

Now, I started to swim out into that tide and the tide suddenly became, felt an extraordinary shove and almost pulling me down again, the water pulling me down and suddenly I realized at that time even as I failed to realize before I dove into the water—that I was in a weakened condition, although as I had looked over that distance between the ferry slip and the other side, it seemed to me an inconsequential swim; but the water got colder, the tide began to draw me out and for the second time that evening, I knew I was going to drown and the strength continued to leave me. By this time I was probably 50 yards off the shore and I remembered being swept down toward the direction of the Edgartown Light and well out into darkness, and I continued to attempt to swim, tried to swim at a slower pace to be able to regain whatever kind of strength that was left in me.

And some time after, I think it was about the middle of the channel, a little further than that, the tide was much calmer, gentler, and I began to get my—make some progress, and finally was able to reach the other shore and all the nightmares and all the tragedy and all the loss of Mary Jo's death was right before me again. And when I was able to gain this shore, this Edgartown side, I pulled myself on the beach and then attempted to gain some strength.

After that I walked up one of the streets in the direction of the Shiretown Inn. By walking up one of the streets I walked into a parking lot that was adjacent to the Inn and I can remember almost having no further strength to continue, and leaning against a tree for a length of time, walking through the parking lot, trying to really gather some kind of idea as to what happened and feeling that I just had to go to my room at that time, which I did by walking through the front entrance of the Shiretown Inn up the stairs.

Q. Do you have any idea what time you arrived at the Shiretown Inn?

A. I would say some time before 2:00.

Q. Can you tell us now how great a distance you swam when you left the ferry slip?

A. I left just adjacent to the ferry slip here, I would say on the north side of it and I was swept down for a number of yards and then across. I don't think I can estimate the terms of the yardage.

Q. When you arrived at the Shiretown Inn, did you talk to anyone at that time?

A. I went to my room and I was shaking with chill. I took off all my clothes and collapsed on the bed, and at this time, I was very conscious of a throbbing headache, of pains in my neck, of strain on my back, but what I was even more conscious of is the tragedy and loss of a very devoted friend.

Q. Now, did you change your clothes?

A. I was unable really to determine, detect the amount of lapse of time and I could hear noise that was taking place. It seemed around me, on top of me, almost in the room, and after a period of time I wasn't sure whether it was morning or afternoon or nighttime, and I put on—and I wanted to find out and I put on some dry clothes that were there a pants and a shirt, and I opened the door and I saw what I believed to be a tourist, someone standing under the light off the balcony and asked what time it was. He mentioned to me it was, I think, 2:30, and went back into the room.

Q. Had you known Miss Kopechne prior to July 18th?

A. Well, I have known her—my family has known her for a number of years. She has visited my house, my wife. She has visited Mrs. Robert Kennedy's house. She worked in the Robert Kennedy Presidential campaign, and I would say that we have known her for a number of years.

Q. Now, directing your—

A. If the question is, have I ever been out with Mary Jo—

Q. No, that is not the question. The question was whether you knew her socially prior to this event.

A. Well, could I give you a fuller explanation of my knowledge of Mary Jo, your Honor?

MR. DINIS: I have no objection.

THE COURT: Go ahead.

THE WITNESS: I have never in my life, as I have stated on television, had any personal relationship with Mary Jo Kopechne. I never in my life have been either out with Mary Jo Kopechne nor have I ever been with her prior to that occasion where we were not in a general assemblage of friends, associates, or members of our family.

Q. (By Mr. Dinis) Directing your attention to the 19th at around 7:30 a.m., did you have any conversation with anyone at that time?

A. Could I hear the question, please?

Q. The 19th, which was that morning at around 7 a.m., 7:30 a.m.—

A. Yes.

Q. Did you meet anyone at your room?

A. Not at 7:30 a.m., I did not.

Q. Did you meet anyone at any time that morning at your room?

A. Yes, I did.

Q. And whom did you meet there?

A. If your Honor would permit me to give—I would like to be specifically responsive, and I can. I think. It might be misleading to the Court if I just gave a specific response to it. Whatever the Court wants.

Q. Well, the point is, what time did you get up that morning?

A. I never really went to bed that night.

Q. I see. After that noise at 2:30 in the morning, when did you first meet anyone, what time?

A. It was sometime after 8.

Q. And whom did you meet?

A. Sometime after 8 I met the woman that was behind the counter at the Shiretown Inn and I met Mr. Richards and Mr. Moore, very briefly Mrs. Richards, and Mr. Gargan and Mr. Markham, and I saw Mr. Treter, but to be specifically responsive as to who I met in my room, which I believe was the earlier question, was Mr. Markham and Mr. Gargan.

Q. What time was this, sometime around 8 o'clock?

A. I think it was close to 8:30.

Q. Did you have any conversation with Mr. Moore or Mrs. Moore or Mr. Richards or Mrs. Richards?

A. It is my impression that they did the talking.

Q. Well, what was the conversation, do you recall?

A. Mr. Moore was relating about how I believe some members of his crew were having difficulty with their housing arrangements.

Q. Now, what time did Mr. Markham and Mr. Gargan arrive?

A. About a few—I would think about 8:30, just a few minutes after I met Mr. Moore probably.

Q. And do you recall how they were dressed?

A. To the best of my knowledge, a shirt and slacks.

Q. Do you recall at this time the condition of their dress?

A. Well, they had an unkempt look about them.

Q. Nothing further, nothing more than that?

A. Well, I mean it was not pressed; it was messy looking. It was unkempt looking.

Q. Did you have any conversation with Mr. Markham or Mr. Gargan or both at that time?

A. Yes, I did.

Q. Can you give the Court what the conversation was?

A. Well, they asked, had I reported the accident, and why I hadn't reported the accident; and I told them about my own thoughts and feelings as I swam across that channel and how I always willed that Mary Jo still lived; how I was hopeful even as that night went on and as I almost tossed and turned, paced that room and walked around that room that night that somehow when they arrived in the morning that they were going to say that Mary Jo was still alive. I told them how I somehow believed that when the sun came up and it was a new morning that what had happened the night before would not have happened and did not happen, and how I just couldn't gain the strength within me, the moral strength to call Mrs. Kopechne at 2 o'clock in the morning and tell her that her daughter was dead.

Q. Now, at some time did you actually call Mrs. Kopechne?

A. Yes, I did.

Q. And prior to calling Mrs. Kopechne, did you cross over on the Chappaquiddick Ferry to Chappaquiddick Island?

A. Yes, I did.

Q. And, was Mr. Markham and Mr. Gargan with you?

A. Yes, they were.

Q. Now, did you then return to Edgartown after some period of time?

A. Yes, I did.

Q. Did anything prompt or cause you to return to Edgartown once you were on Chappaquiddick Island that morning?

A. Anything prompt me to? Well, what do you mean by prompt?

Q. Well, did anything cause you to return? You crossed over to Chappaquiddick?

A. Other than the intention of reporting the accident, the intention of which had been made earlier that morning.

Q. But you didn't go directly from your room to the police department?

A. No, I did not.

Q. Did you have a particular reason for going to Chappaquiddick first?

A. Yes, I did.

Q. What was that reason?

A. It was to make a private phone call to one of the dearest and oldest friends that I have and that was to Mr. Burke Marshall. I didn't feel that I could use the phone that was available outside of the dining room at the Shiretown Inn, and it was my thought that once I went to the police station, that I would be involved in a myriad of details and I wanted to talk to this friend before I undertook that responsibility.

Q. You mean that—

THE COURT: Excuse me, Mr. Dinis, we are now at 1 o'clock.

MR. DINIS: The recess.

THE COURT: I think we will take the noon luncheon recess.

AFTERNOON SESSION

THE COURT: All right, Mr. Dinis.

Q. (By Mr. Dinis) Mr. Kennedy, you said that you made a phone call to a friend, Mr. Burke Marshall?

A. I made a phone call with the intention of reaching Mr. Burke Marshall.

Q. You did not reach him?

A. No, I did not.

Q. And then I believe the evidence is that you left Chappaquiddick Island, crossed over on the ferry and went over to the local police department?

A. That is correct.

Q. There you made a report to Chief Arena?

A. That is right.

Q. And you arrived at the police station at approximately 10 a.m.?

A. I think it was sometime before 10.

Q. And you made a statement in writing, is that correct?

A. That is correct.

Q. Did the chief reduce this to a typewritten statement, do you know?

A. No, he did not.

Q. Now, I have in my hand what purports to be the statement that you made to Chief Arena at that time, and I would like to give you a copy of that, and in this statement you saw—well, would you read it first, Senator?

A. Yes, that is correct.

Q. Now, Senator, prior to the phone call you made, the effort you made to contact Burke Marshall by phone, did you make any other phone calls?

A. Yes, I did.

Q. Where did you make these phone calls?

A. I made one call after 8 o'clock in the morning from the public phone outside of the restaurant at the Shiretown Inn.

Q. One call?

A. That is all. This was made sometime after 8.

Q. And to whom did you make this call?

A. I was attempting to reach Mr. Stephen Smith, the party that I felt would know the number.

Q. Were you alone in the police station?

A. No. At certain times I was, but if the thrust of the question is did I arrive at the police station with someone with me, I did.

Q. And who was that?

A. Mr. Markham.

Q. Mr. Markham.

A. Yes.

Q. With regard to the statement that you made at the police station, Senator, you wind up saying, "When I fully realized what had happened this morning, I immediately contacted the police." Now is that in fact what you did?

THE COURT: Mr. Dinis, are you going to ask the statement be put in the record?

MR. DINIS: Yes, your Honor.

THE COURT: Mr. Kennedy already said this was a copy of the statement he made. He already testified as to all his movements. Now, won't you let the record speak for itself?

MR. DINIS: All right, your Honor.

THE COURT: This will be Exhibit—

MR. TELLER: 2.

THE COURT: 2.

(Statement given to Chief Arena by Senator Kennedy marked Exhibit 2.)

Q. (By Mr. Dinis) Senator, you testified earlier that when you arrived at the cottage you asked Mr. LaRosa to tell Mr. Markham you were outdoors, outside of the house, when you arrived back at the house?

A. No, that is not correct.

Q. Did you ask someone to call Mr. Markham?

A. I asked Joe Gargan when he entered the vehicle to call for Mr. Markham.

Q. Well, did you at that time ask anyone to take you back to Edgartown at that time when you arrived back at the house after the accident?

A. No. I asked Mr. Gargan to go to the scene of the accident.

Q. But you didn't ask anyone to take you directly back to Edgartown?

A. I asked them to take me to Edgartown after their diving.

Q. After the diving?

A. After their diving.

Q. I show you, Mr. Kennedy, what purports to be a copy of the televised broadcast which you made approximately a week after the accident. Would you read the statement and tell me whether or not this is an exact copy of what you said?

A. (Witness complied) Yes. After a quick reading of it, I would say that that is accurate.

MR. DINIS: Your Honor, may I introduce this statement made by Senator Kennedy in a televised broadcast?

THE COURT: You may, Exhibit No. 3. (Statement made by Senator Kennedy in televised broadcast marked Exhibit 3.)

Q. Now, Senator in that televised broadcast you said and I quote, "I instructed Gargan and Markham not to alarm Mary Jo's friends that night," is that correct?

A. That is correct. I would like to—

Q. Look at it?

A. —look at it. I believe that is correct.

Q. It would be on page 3.

(Witness examined the document.)

A. That is correct.

Q. Can you tell the Court what prompted you to give this instruction to Markham and Gargan?

A. Yes, I can.

Q. Will you do that, please?

A. I felt strongly that if those girls were notified that an accident had taken place and that Mary Jo had in fact drowned, which I became convinced of by the time that Markham and Gargan and I left the scene of the accident, that it would only be a matter of seconds before all of those girls who were long and dear friends of Mary Jo's to go to the scene of the accident and dive themselves and enter the water with, I felt, a good chance that some serious mishap might have occurred to any one of them. It was for that reason that I restrained—asked Mr. Gargan and Mr. Markham not to alarm the girls.

MR. DINIS: I have no further questions of Mr. Kennedy.

THE COURT: And I have no further questions. Would you be available in the event we needed you back for anything?

THE WITNESS: I will make myself available, your Honor.

THE COURT: Well, were you planning to stay in Hyannis Port or some place near?

THE WITNESS: Well, I will. I will be glad to be available.

THE COURT: Otherwise you would go back to Boston?

THE WITNESS: No, I would return to Cape Cod tonight and I would hope to be able to return to Washington sometime this week, but I would be glad to remain available to the Court if the Court so desired.

THE COURT: Well, it is difficult for me to say right now.

THE WITNESS: Well, then, I will remain available as long as—

THE COURT: We will try to give you as much notice as possible if we felt it essential to have you back.

MR. DINIS: Your Honor, I think we could make it an overnight notice, so if the Senator had to be in Washington, we would arrange for his arrival the next day, if necessary, which may not be.

THE COURT: All right, subject to that, you are excused.

THE WITNESS: Your Honor, could I talk to my counsel before being released, just on one point that I might like to address the bench on?

THE COURT: Go ahead.

(Off the record discussion between Mr. Kennedy and lawyers.)

THE COURT: And I think we can put in the record this question. Why did you not seek further assistance after Mr. Markham and Mr. Gargan had exhausted their efforts in attempting to reach Mary Jo? Now, you give the answer.

THE WITNESS: It is because I was completely convinced at that time that no further help and assistance would do Mary Jo any more good. I realized that she must be drowned and still in the car at this time, and it appeared the question in my mind at that time was, what should be done about the accident.

THE COURT: Anything further? Off the record.

(Discussion off the record.)

THE COURT: All right, take this.

THE WITNESS: Since the alcoholic intake is relevant; there is one further question, your Honor, and although I haven't been asked it, I feel that in all frankness and fairness and for a complete record that it should be included as a part of the complete proceedings, and that is that during the course of the race that afternoon that there were two other members of my crew and I shared what would be two beers between us at different points in the race, and one other occasion in which there was some modest intake of alcohol would be after the race at the slip in which Ross Richards' boat was attached, moored, that I shared a beer with Mr. John Driscoll. The sum and substance of that beer would be, I think, less than a quarter of one, but I felt that for the complete record that at least the Court should at least be aware of these instances as well.

THE COURT: Anything more?

THE WITNESS: There is nothing further.

THE COURT: Anything more, Mr. Dinis?

MR. DINIS: No, your Honor.

THE COURT: All right, you are excused subject to further recall. Off the record.

(Discussion off the record.)

THE COURT: All right, your next witness, Mr. Dinis.

JUDGE BOYLE'S REPORT

JUDGE BOYLE'S HANDLING of the police court guilty plea and the later inquest have been both attacked and defended. Here is his inquest report. Judge Boyle could have forced prosecution in this case—but he didn't do it.

COMMONWEALTH OF MASSACHUSETTS

Dukes County, ss

District Court
Inquest re Mary Jo Kopechne
Docket No. 15220

REPORT
James A. Boyle, Justice

I, James A. Boyle, Justice of the District Court for the County of Dukes County, in performance of the duty required of me by Section 12 of Chapter 38 of the General Laws of Massachusetts, in the matter of the inquest into the death of Mary Jo Kopechne, holden at Edgartown January 5, 1970 to January 8, 1970 inclusive, herewith submit my report.

There are 763 pages of transcript and 33 numbered exhibits. Although most testimony was given orally, some was accepted by affidavit and included as exhibits.

It is believed that, to aid in understanding this report, certain names and places should first be relatively located and some measurements shown:

(1)   The town of Edgartown, which is one of six towns on Martha's Vineyard, includes a small, sparsely settled island named Chappaquiddick. (Map, Exhibit 32)

(2)   The mainland of Edgartown is separated from Chappaquiddick by Edgartown Harbor, the distance between being approximately five hundred feet, and transportation of vehicles and persons is provided by a small motor ferry which plies two ferry slips or landings. The ferry slip on the Edgartown side is near the center of town. (Exhibit 19)

(3)   Chappaquiddick has few roads. At the ferry slip, begins a macadam paved road called Chappaquiddick Road, the main road of the island, with a white center line which is partly obliterated at the curve. The road is approximately 20 feet wide, running in a general easterly direction for two and one-half miles, whence it curves south and continues in that direction past the cottage to the southeast corner of the island. Chappaquiddick Road is sometimes referred to in the testimony as Main Street and, after it curves, as School Road or Schoolhouse Road, because a schoolhouse formerly stood on that portion of it. (Exhibits 16, 19)

(4)   At the curve, and continuing easterly, begins Dyke Road, a dirt and sand road, seventeen to nineteen feet wide, which runs a distance of seven-tenths miles to Dyke Bridge, shortly beyond which is the ocean beach. (Exhibits 15, 16, 17)

(5)   Dyke Bridge is a wooden structure, ten feet, six inches wide, has timber curbs on each side four inches high by ten inches wide, no other guard rails, and runs at an angle of twenty-seven degrees to the left of the road. There are no signs or artificial lights on the bridge or its approach. It spans Poucha Pond. (Exhibits 7, 8, 9, 10)

(6)   The Kennedy Oldsmobile is eighteen feet long and eighty inches wide. (Exhibits 1, 33)

(7)   Poucha Pond is a salt water tidal pond, and has a strong current where it narrows at Dyke Bridge. (Exhibits 10, 18)

(8)   Cemetery Road is a single car-width private dirt road, which runs northerly from the junction of Chappaquiddick and Dyke Roads. (Exhibits 16, 22)

(9)   The Lawrence Cottage (herein called Cottage) is one-half mile from the junction of Chappaquiddick and Dyke Roads

and approximately three miles from the ferry slip. (Exhibit 20)

(10)   Proceeding northerly from the Cottage, on the east side of Chappaquiddick Road, a distance of one-tenth mile before the curve, is a metal sign with an arrow pointing toward the ferry landing.

(11)   Katama Shores Motor Inn (called Katama Shores) is located approximately two miles from the Edgartown ferry slip.

(12)   Shiretown Inn (called Shiretown) is a very short distance from the Edgartown ferry slip, approximately one block.

Although the testimony is not wholly consistent, a general summary of the material circumstances is this: A group of twelve persons, by invitation of Edward M. Kennedy, a United States Senator from Massachusetts, were gathered together at Edgartown to attend the annual sailing regatta held on Friday and Saturday, July 18 and 19, 1969. They were:

John B. Crimmins	Rosemary Keough
Joseph Gargan	Mary Jo Kopechne
Edward M. Kennedy	Ann (also called Nance) Lyons
Raymond S. LaRosa	Maryellen Lyons
Paul F. Markham	Esther Newburgh
Charles C. Tretter	Susan Tannenbaum

(All hereafter referred to by surnames)

The six young women, in their twenties, had been associated together in Washington, D.C. and were quite close friends. Kopechne shared a Washington apartment with Ann Lyons. Reservations had been made for them to stay at Katama Shores, in three double rooms. Kopechne roomed with Newburgh. Crimmins, chauffeur for Kennedy when he was in Massachusetts, drove Kennedy's black Oldsmobile sedan from Boston to Martha's Vineyard on Wednesday, July 16. He brought a supply of liquor with him and stayed at the Cottage. Tretter, who brought some of the young women, arrived late Thursday and stayed at Shiretown. LaRosa, who brought his Mercury car, came Thursday and shared the room with Tretter. Gargan and Markham sailed Kennedy's boat to Edgartown on Thursday and roomed together at Shiretown. Kennedy arrived by plane on Friday, July 18, was met by Crimmins at the airport, and was driven to the Cottage. Kennedy shared a room at Shiretown with Gargan. The Lyons sisters arrived Friday morning and were driven by Gargan to Katama Shores. Markham, who stayed at Shiretown Thursday night, moved to the Cottage to stay with Crimmins for Friday and Saturday nights. Kennedy, with Gargan, was entered to sail his boat in the regatta on Friday and Saturday.

The Cottage became headquarters for the group and a cook-out was planned for Friday night. Three cars were available for general transportation; LaRosa's Mercury, Kennedy's Oldsmobile 88, and a rented white Valiant.

Thursday night those present, including Kopechne, visited the Cottage; Friday morning, they, including Kopechne, traveled over Dyke Bridge to the beach to swim; Friday evening, they, including Kopechne, traveled to the Cottage for the cook-out. Kennedy who arrived at 1:00 p.m. Friday and was driven by Crimmins to the Cottage, was then driven by Crimmins over Dyke Road and Dyke Bridge to the beach to swim; he was driven back to the Cottage to change, to the ferry slip to sail in the race, and, after the race, was driven back to the Cottage. There were other trips between Edgartown and the Cottage, but not including Kopechne or Kennedy. These are set forth to indicate the use of, and increasing familiarity with, the roads of Chappaquiddick.

The Cottage is small, contains a combination kitchen-living room, two bedrooms and bath, has an open yard, no telephone, and is near to and visible from Chappaquiddick Road, which had little traffic. The entire group of twelve had assembled there by approximately 8:30 p.m. on Friday. Two cars were available for transportation on Chappaquiddick, the Oldsmobile and Valiant. LaRosa's Mercury was at the Shiretown. Activities consisted of cooking, eating, drinking, conversation, singing and dancing. Available alcoholic beverages consisted of vodka, rum, scotch, and beer. There was not much drinking and no one admitted to more than three drinks; most only to two or less.

During the evening, Tretter, with Keough, drove to Edgartown in the Oldsmobile to borrow a radio. Keough left her pocketbook in the vehicle on that trip.

Only Crimmins and Markham planned to stay the night at the Cottage. The others intended to return to their respective hotels in Edgartown. It was known that the last ferry trip was about midnight, but that a special arrangement for a later trip could be made.

Between 11:15 and 11:30 p.m., Kennedy told Crimmins (but no other person) that he was tired, wanted to return to Shiretown to bed, that Kopechne did not feel well (some conflict here—see pages 32 and 346) [page numbers refer to Inquest Record—Author] and he was taking her back to Katama Shores, requested and obtained the car keys to the Oldsmobile, and both he and Kopechne departed. Kopechne told no one, other than Kennedy, that she was leaving. Kopechne left her pocketbook at the Cottage.

Kennedy stated he drove down Chappaquiddick Road toward the ferry, that when he reached the junction of Dyke Road, instead of bearing left on the Curve to continue on Chappaquiddick Road, he mistakenly turned right onto Dyke Road, realized at some point he was on a dirt road, but thought nothing of it, was proceeding at about twenty miles per hour when suddenly Dyke Bridge was upon him. He braked but the car went off the bridge into Poucha Pond and landed on its roof. The driver's window was open and he managed to reach the surface and swim to shore. It was extremely dark, there was a strong current, and repeated efforts by him to extricate Kopechne from the car were unsuccessful. Exhausted, he went to shore and, when recovered, walked back to the Cottage, not noticing any lights or houses on the way. He summoned Gargan and Markham, without notifying the others, and they returned in the Valiant to the bridge, where Gargan and Markham unsuccessfully attempted to recover Kopechne.

The three drove back to the ferry landing. After much discussion, it was decided that Kennedy would return to Edgartown (no mention how) to telephone David Burke, his administrative assistant, and Burke Marshall, an attorney, and then report the accident to the police. Kennedy advised Gargan and Markham to return to the Cottage, but not to tell the others of the accident. Suddenly and unexpectedly, Kennedy left the car, dove into the harbor and swam across to Edgartown. Gargan and Markham finally returned to the Cottage, but did not then tell the others what had occurred.

After Kennedy and Kopechne had left the Cottage, their purported destination unknown to anyone except Crimmins, the social activities gradually diminished. The absence of Kennedy and Kopechne was noticed but it was presumed they had returned to Edgartown. Some persons went walking. Only LaRosa saw Kennedy return at about 12:30 a.m. and he, at Kennedy's request, summoned Gargan and Markham, who went to Kennedy, seated outside in the rear seat of the Valiant, and they took off. When Markham and Gargan returned about 2:00 a.m., some were sleeping and the others, realizing they would not return to Edgartown that night, then slept or tried to. There not being sufficient beds, some slept on the floor.

In the morning, those in the Cottage returned to Edgartown at different times. The young women eventually reached Katama Shores and were then told what had happened, although some of them had previously been made aware that Kopechne was missing.

Kennedy, after swimming across to Edgartown, went to his room, took off his wet clothes, lay on the bed, then dressed, went outside and complained to someone (later identified as the innkeeper, Russell Peachy) of noise and to inquire the time. He was told it was 2:24 a.m. He returned to his room and remained there until 7:30 a.m. when he went outside, met Richards, a sailing competitor, chatted with him for one-half hour, when Gargan and Markham appeared and the three retired to Kennedy's room. When Kennedy informed them he had failed to report the accident, they all went to Chappaquiddick to use the public telephone near the ferry slip and Kennedy called David Burke, his administrative assistant, in Washington. (But Exhibit 4, list of calls charged to Kennedy, does not show this call.) Gargan returned to the Cottage to tell those there about the accident. Kennedy and Markham went to the Edgartown Police Station, and were later joined by Gargan.

At about 8:20 a.m. Police Chief Arena, receiving notice of a submerged car at Dyke Bridge, hurried to the scene, changed into swim trunks, and made several futile attempts to enter the Oldsmobile. Farrar, a scuba diver, was summoned, found and recovered the body of Kopechne from the car, and also found in the car the pocketbook of Keough. The car was later towed to shore.

Dr. Donald R. Mills of Edgartown, Associate Medical Examiner, was summoned and arrived about 9:15 a.m., examined the body and pronounced death by drowning, and turned it over to Eugene Frieh, a mortician, who took the body to his establishment at Vineyard Haven. The clothing and a sample of blood from the body were turned over to the State Police for analysis. No autopsy was performed and the body was embalmed and flown to Pennsylvania on Sunday for burial.

When Kennedy and Markham arrived at the Police Station, Chief Arena was at Dyke Bridge. He returned to the station at Kennedy's request. Kennedy stated he was the operator of the car and dictated a statement of the accident as Markham wrote it down. Chief Arena then typed the statement which Kennedy said was correct but did not sign. (Exhibit 2)

On July 25, 1969, Kennedy pleaded guilty in this Court to, and was sentenced on, a criminal charge of "leaving the scene of an accident after causing personal injury, without making himself known." That same night, Kennedy made a television statement to the voters of Massachusetts. (Exhibit 3)

A petition by District Attorney Edmund Dinis in the Court of Common Pleas for Luzerne County, Pennsylvania, for exhumation and autopsy on the body of Kopechne, was denied after hearing. Expert evidence was introduced that chemical analysis of the blouse worn by Kopechne showed blood stains, but medical evidence proved this was not inconsistent with death by drowning. (Exhibit 31)

Christopher F. Look, Jr., a deputy sheriff then living on Chappaquiddick, was driving easterly on Chappaquiddick Road to his home about 12:45 A.M. on July 19. As he approached the junction of Dyke Road, a car crossed in front of him and entered Cemetery Road, stopped, backed up, and drove easterly on Dyke Road. He saw two persons in the front seat, a shadow on the shelf back of the rear seat which he thought could have been a bag, article of clothing or a third person. The car was dark colored with Massachusetts registration plate L7 - 7. He was unable to remember any other numbers or how many there were intervening. Later that morning, he saw the Kennedy Oldsmobile when it was towed to shore, but he cannot positively identify it as the same car he saw at 12:45 A.M. During the inquest, a preliminary investigation was initiated through the Registry of Motor Vehicles to determine whether a tracking of the location on July 18 and 19, 1969, of all dark colored cars bearing Massachusetts plates with any and all combinations of numbers beginning with L7 and ending in 7, would be practicable. The attempt was disclosed that it would not be feasible to do this since there would be no assurance that the end result would be helpful and, in any event, the elimination of all other cars within that registration group (although it would seriously affect the credibility of some of the witnesses) would not alter the findings of this report.

A short distance before Dyke Bridge, there is a small house called "Dyke House", then occupied by a Mrs. Malm and her daughter. (Exhibit 18) Both heard a car sometime before midnight but are not sure of its direction. The daughter turned off her light at midnight. (Page 593 et seq.)

Drs. Watt and Brougham examined Kennedy on July 19 and 22. Diagnostic opinion was "concussion, contusions and abrasions of the scalp, acute cervical strain. Impairment of judgement and confused behavior are consistent with this type of injury." (Exhibit 27)

Eugene D. Jones, a professional engineer, testified by affidavit as to the condition of Dyke Road and Dyke Bridge and concluded that the site is well below approved engineering standards and particularly hazardous at night. (Exhibits 29, 30)

Donald L. Sullivan, an employee of Arthur D. Little, Inc. testified by affidavit as to a road test conducted on or about October 10, 1969, describing the factors involved in a motor vehicle, on high beam light, approaching Dyke Bridge at night, with film showing the results of such test. (Exhibit 28)

State Police Chemist McHugh, who analyzed the blood sample taken from the body of Kopechne, testified the alcoholic content was .09 percent, the equivalent of three and one-half to five ounces of eighty to ninety proof liquor consumed by a person, weighing about one hundred ten pounds, within an hour prior to death, or a larger amount if consumed within a longer period.

This concluded in substance, the material circumstances as testified to by the witnesses.

The failure of Kennedy to seek additional assistance in searching for Kopechne, whether excused by his condition, or whether or not it would have been of any material help, has not been pursued because such failure, even when shown, does not constitute criminal conduct.

Since there was no evidence that any air remained in the immersed car, testimony was not sought or allowed concerning how long Kopechne might have lived, had such a condition existed, as this could only be conjecture and purely speculative.

As previously stated, there are inconsistencies and contradictions in the testimony, which a comparison of individual testimony will show. It is not feasible to attempt to indicate each one.

I list my findings as follows:

I.   The decedent is Mary Jo Kopechne, 28 years of age, last resident in Washington, D.C.

II. Death probably occurred between 11:30 P.M. on July 18, 1969 and 1:00 A.M. on July 19, 1969.

III. Death was caused by drowning in Poucha Pond at Dyke Bridge on Chappaquiddick Island in the Town of Edgartown, Massachusetts, when a motor vehicle, in which the decedent was a passenger, went off Dyke Bridge, overturned and was immersed in Poucha Pond. The motor vehicle was owned and operated by Edward M. Kennedy of Boston, Massachusetts.

The statute states that I must report the name of any person whose unlawful act or negligence *appears* to have contributed to Kopechne's death. As I stated at the commencement of the hearing, the Massachusetts Supreme Court said in its decision concerning the conduct of this inquest, "the inquest serves as an aid in the achievement of justice by obtaining information as to whether a crime has been committed." In *LaChappelle vs. United Shoes Machinery Corporation*, 318 Mass. 166, decided in 1945, the same Court said "It is designed merely to ascertain facts for the purpose of subsequent prosecution"and ". . . the investigating judge may himself issue process against a person whose *probable* guilt is disclosed." (Emphasis added)

Therefore, in guiding myself as to the proof herein required of the commission of any unlawful act, I reject the cardinal principle of "proof beyond a reasonable doubt" applied in criminal trials but use as a standard the principle of "probable guilt".

I have also used the rule, applicable to trials, which permits me to draw inferences, known as presumption of facts, from the testimony. There are several definitions and I quote from the case of *Commonwealth vs. Green,* 295 Pa. 573: "A presumption of fact is an inference which a reasonable man would draw from certain facts which have been proven. The basis is in logic and its source of probability." Volume 29 *American Jurisprudence,* 2nd Evidence Section 161 states in part, "A presumption of fact or an inference is nothing more than a probable or natural explanation of facts . . . and arises from the commonly accepted experiences of mankind and the inference which reasonable men would draw from experiences."

I find these facts:

A. Kennedy was the host and mainly responsible for the assembly of the group at Edgartown.

B. Kennedy was rooming at Shiretown with Gargan, his cousin and close friend of many years.

C. Kennedy had employed Crimmins as Chauffeur for nine years and rarely drove himself. Crimmins drove Kennedy on all other occasions herein set forth, and was available at the time of the fatal trip.

D. Kennedy told only Crimmins that he was leaving for Shiretown and requested the car keys.

E. The young women were close friends, were on Martha's

Vineyard for a common purpose as a cohesive group, and staying together at Katama Shores.

F. Kopechne roomed with Newburgh, the latter having in her possession the key to their room.

G. Kopechne told no one, other than Kennedy that she was leaving for Katama Shores and did not ask Newburgh for the room key.

H. Kopechne left her pocketbook at the Cottage when she drove off with Kennedy.

I. It was known that the ferry ceased operation about midnight and special arrangements must be made for a later trip. No such arrangements were made.

J. Ten of the persons at the cook-out did not intend to remain at the Cottage overnight.

K. Only the Oldsmobile and the Valiant were available for transportation of those ten, the Valiant being the smaller car.

L. LaRosa's Mercury was parked at Shiretown and was available for use.

I infer a reasonable and probable explanation of the totality of the above facts is that Kennedy and Kopechne did not intend to return to Edgartown at that time; that Kennedy did not intend to drive to the ferry slip and his turn onto Dyke Road was intentional. Having reached this conclusion, the question then arises as to whether there was anything criminal in his operation of the motor vehicle.

From two personal views, which corroborate the Engineer's statement (Exhibit 29), and other evidence, I am fully convinced that Dyke Bridge constitutes a traffic hazard, particularly so at night, and must be approached with extreme caution. A speed of even twenty miles per hour, as Kennedy testified to, operating a car as large as this Oldsmobile, would at least be negligent and, possibly, reckless. If Kennedy knew of this hazard, his operation of the vehicle constituted criminal conduct.

Earlier on July 18, he had been driven over Chappaquiddick Road three times, and over Dyke Road and Dyke Bridge twice. Kopechne had been driven over Chappaquiddick Road five times and over Dyke Road and Dyke Bridge twice.

I believe it probable that Kennedy knew of this hazard that lay ahead of him on Dyke Road but that, for some reason not apparent from the testimony, he failed to exercise due care as he approached the bridge.

IV. I, therefore, find there is probably cause to believe that Edward M. Kennedy operated his motor vehicle negligently in a way or in a place to which the public have a right of access and that such operation appears to have contributed to the death of Mary Jo Kopechne.

February 18, 1970

JAMES A. BOYLE
Justice

THE NOT-SO-GRAND JURY

FROM WHAT SEEMED a cast of clowns and scoundrels emerged Leslie Leland, the foreman of the Grand Jury holding sessions in Dukes County, Massachusetts. He was a modern day Don Quixote looking for windmills, bridges and possibly a Senator.

Leland, like many others in Massachusetts, believed that the law should be applied uniformly to all. He felt Senator Kennedy had made a mockery of the law, Massachusetts and Edgartown. Leland was disturbed at the outcry, criticism and the unfavorable publicity directed towards his beloved Bay State because of the Kennedy case.

From the beginning, Leland had repeatedly urged District Attorney Dinis to bring the matter before the grand jury. He felt his pleas for justice fell on deaf ears. Leland even asked Attorney General Quinn of Massachusetts whether he (Leland) could call a special session of the grand jury, but was told it would be illegal.

What appeared to be behind-the-scenes protection for the Senator went on for months, blocking Leland at every turn. During this time, the Senator had pleaded guilty to a minor traffic charge and had been slapped on the wrist—but he had never been questioned as to what had happened. A young girl was dead, but Chief Arena hadn't even asked Kennedy if he had been drinking!

Leland saw the Kennedy case take many strange turns. It seemed incomprehensible that the Kopechnes had joined in blocking the autopsy which could have answered all the major questions about how, when and why their daughter had died. Leland questioned the value of the inquest which had been held under rules that destroyed any value it might have had.

Since justice appeared to be getting bushwhacked instead of served, Leland pulled out his ace in the hole, the grand jury, the historic weapon of the people. Its powers were more than adequate to investigate every aspect of the Chappaquiddick affair if Leland could only get it started.

Leland finally became fed up with those the reporters had dubbed "Teddy Hacks". Towards the end of March, 1970, Leland directed a letter to the highest individual legal authority in the state, His Honor, the Chief Justice of the Massachusetts Supreme Court. Leland asked that his grand jury be especially convened to investigate Chappaquiddick and particularly to look over the transcript of the inquest proceedings. Immediately, the Chief Justice denied ever receiving such a letter. Not knowing whether the Judge was bluffing or lying, Leland publicly exhibited the judge's signature on the receipt for Leland's registered letter sent to that (as some say) "Supremely Courted Chief Justice". Leland was immediately granted a special session of the grand jury on April 6.

The Kennedy forces regrouped because the grand jury situation began to look serious. Leland couldn't take a hint, so they had to find another way to fend off this determined but misguided man. This chore was delegated to Judge Wilfred J. Pacquet of the Massachusetts Superior Court. Conveniently, Pacquet was the judge into whose custody the inquest records had been remanded.

Judge Pacquet executed his commission with complete efficiency. He called the members of the grand jury into his court to "instruct" them as to their duties. For over an hour he intimidated them in the best Salem tradition. He warned them and threatened them with the terrible things that would happen to the jurors personally if they disobeyed any of his injunctions, including that they would be sent to jail.

He continually browbeat them and branded the scarlet "S" of secrecy in their minds. Pacquet instructed them never to disclose the nature of their deliberations or the names of any of the witnesses. ". . . and I don't mean for a day," the judge said, "I mean forever. Your lips are sealed."[1] To help convince the grand jurors, the judge had a priest on the bench with him. The latter provided, free of charge, a few prayers designed to invoke charity to replace prejudice.

[1] *Human Events,* April 18, 1970.

The judge did everything but physically pull a gun on the members of that ill-fated grand jury. He gave them the horse to ride and immediately shot it out from under them. Pacquet told them they could summon and question any witnesses that could give "useful information", but they would not be permitted to see the inquest transcript nor could they question the inquest witnesses. This wrapped up the package, and the show was, for all practical purposes, over.

The Chicago *Tribune* said: "This remarkable ruling, depriving the grand jury of access to the record, amounted to a directive to the District Attorney to pledge that there would be no prosecution of Sen. Kennedy .... The Senator has been given special benefits and kid glove treatment from every court before which he has been represented."

Judge Pacquet was a real operator, he got results. The grand jury was dead. If the jurors obeyed Judge Pacquet's orders—and what else could they do—there was literally no evidence available on Chappaquiddick that they could hear. If they disobeyed him they went to jail. It was not a very wide choice, but quite effective.

After 45 minutes, the grand jury gave up the ghost and reported to Judge Pacquet that they had no indictments to present. It was no surprise to anyone—certainly not Judge Pacquet and Senator Kennedy—that Leland and his grand jury announced "We have no presentment to make."

The Chicago *Tribune* said: "Events—with a certain amount of assistance from courts and public officials who were either negligent or partisan—have certainly conspired to protect Sen. Kennedy at every turn in this strange sequence. Now the sudden abandonment of the grand jury investigation indicates what has been a virtual certainty from the beginning— that the true facts of the episode will forever remain veiled." Usually, justice triumphs at the end of a courtroom scene. In this case the Kennedy forces buried it along with Mary Jo and the public's right to know the truth about Chappaquiddick.

In order to fully comprehend the extent of the obstruction of justice in this case, let us briefly review what constitutes a grand jury.

The judicial body known as a grand jury dates back many centuries into early English history, its origins now lost in obscurity. The grand jury came into being to protect the subjects, the common people, from oppression and injustice perpetrated by the Crown, the Establishment if you prefer. It has been a bulwark against abuses of power by the sovereign for hundreds of years. There is nothing mysterious or complicated about a grand jury; it is one of the cornerstones of our society.

The grand jury guards the rights and liberties of the public and protects its morals and social order. In the fearless exercise of its powers, and the necessary incidents thereto, the grand jury is not to be limited or circumscribed by any judicial or executive officer. Nor is it to be subjected to outside influence of any kind; neither judges, nor governors nor presidents.

The grand jury calls for such witnesses and evidence as required in fulfilling its duties. No court or person has any right to interfere in its functions. Any such interference is a violation of law.

The aforementioned facts are considered by the legal profession to be "Hornbook Law", elementary basic legal principles. In this case, Judge Pacquet destroyed the grand jury and everything it stood for.

Some of the proceedings in the Massachusetts courts and/or by Massachusetts judges are hard to follow and harder to agree with. If the handling of the present case is considered to be standard, then one can only say with heartfelt sincerity that the Good Lord please help the parties litigant in cases pending in the courts of Massachusetts. It seems obvious that they aren't going to obtain justice by anything short of Divine Intervention.

Part Three

The Search For Truth

BEHIND CLOSED DOORS

CHAPPAQUIDDICK IS THE MOST TALKED ABOUT CASE in contemporary times, and probably the most discussed traffic accident in history. The death of Mary Jo Kopechne has prompted a large number of claims and theories. The "real" cause of death ranges from drowning to murder. It is essential to clear the air and separate fact from fiction in order to understand the case and the answers properly. Senator Kennedy has only himself to blame for this maze of confusion and the wide-ranging accusations. If he had called the police and told the complete story at the time of the accident, it would have been over years ago.

It is important to review the various Chappaquiddick theories in an effort to alleviate unnecessary confusion. In his book, *The Bridge at Chappaquiddick,* Jack Olsen states his belief that Senator Kennedy was not in the car when it went off the bridge (pp. 241 et seq.). The Senator was alarmed that Deputy Sheriff Look had seen him in a questionable situation, so he got out of the car to hide, telling Mary Jo to drive to the beach and circle around to pick him up if the police did not follow her. She, being unfamiliar with the road, the big car and the bridge, accidentally drove off the bridge alone. The Senator did not learn about the accident until the morning.

We believe this theory is off-base for a number of reasons. First of all, if it was the truth, the Senator would have been a lot better off coming clean than inventing a story that he was in shock for nine hours. Also, at that time, no Kennedy had had any trouble with the police or press for years, and certainly not with any Massachusetts policemen. Olsen wrote that book before the inquest. In the last several years many facts have come out which refute his thesis.

Burton Hersh, author of *The Education of Edward Kennedy*, indulges in no theories as such. He is satisfied that Kennedy lied. Hersh says that the Senator knowingly took Dyke Road so that he and Mary Jo could be alone on the beach. Kennedy did not see the bridge in time and drove off. The rest pretty much fits the Senator's line. (pp. 384, 397)

Zad Rust, author of *Teddy Bare,* believes these were the callous actions of a man involved in an international conspiracy of power. Rust feels that the lack of an autopsy, which Kennedy prevented, leaves a possible American Tragedy situation involving the death before "drowning" of a pregnant Mary Jo. With the body in the car, Kennedy pulled a stunt man routine, jumping out of the car and onto the bridge as the car sank into Poucha Pond (p. 24 et seq.). Rust may be right in that there is a possibility that Kennedy killed Mary Jo because she was pregnant, but we don't think it a substantial one in these days of casual sex, the pill and easy abortions. It is a little too dramatic for us even though the Senator hid the evidence that would disprove it.

The followers of Camelot have been right in there pitching to counterbalance the "sacrilegious" theories: Lester David, with *Ted Kennedy: Triumphs and Tragedies,* and William Honan, with *Ted Kennedy: Profile of a Survivor.* These boys are True Believers, and feel that Teddy's television "testament" is gospel second to none, including the King James Bible.

Robert Sherrill wrote a lengthy article for *The New York Times Magazine,* "Chappaquiddick + 5". Sherrill scrupulously details all of the evidence pro and con and is satisfied that Kennedy lied about the time of the accident and the destination. He seems only mildly undecided as to whether the Senator was drunk or sober when the car went off the bridge and shows no interest at all in any of the far-out theories.

Jack Anderson and *Time* magazine both question the details of time and destination, but basically accept the accident as such. Both raise the point of whether the delay in reporting the accident was occasioned by the arrangements being made with Kennedy's cousin, Joe Gargan, to take the rap as driver of the car. *Time* mentions another theory that the delay was caused by Senator Kennedy needing the time to sober up.

Human Events, which has continuously pointed out the contradictions in Senator Kennedy's story from the beginning, printed a special supplement on November 2, 1974, by David Franke. Franke does not believe Kennedy on all his claims of the time and destination but accepts the accident as such. His greatest concern seems to be with the delay in reporting the matter to the police, and whether Mary Jo might have been saved.

The Republican National Committee paper on Chappaquiddick notes several of the above theories and more. It refers to the one where Mary Jo (sleepy or drunk) left the cottage and got into the back seat of the car and fell asleep. Later Kennedy and Rosemary Keough went for a ride to the beach unaware of her presence. When the car went off the bridge, they were both able to get out, swam ashore and left, still unaware of Mary Jo in the back seat. This would explain Miss Keough's purse found in the submerged car.

Though this theory is supposedly from anonymous sources, we think it was inspired and planted on behalf of the Senator, as it is highly favorable to him. We have run into it several times from pro-Kennedy people. If the theory were true, there would be no possible reason to conceal it as it would be the best "defense" available here. It would also completely remove the great moral taint from the very worst aspect of the case: Kennedy's failure to call authorities to help Mary Jo. We are satisfied there is no truth in this one.

That same paper also mentions the rumor that the car was in fact driven by Joseph Kennedy III, the Senator's nephew. Since the boy was only a minor, Uncle Ted decided to accept the blame to protect young Joe. Our only comment here is, that will be the day!

Many variations on the pregnancy theory abound, and only an autopsy would have settled it either way. Though Kennedy regrets this type of speculation, it is his own fault for covering up the truth.

It is interesting to note that *none,* repeat *none* of the sponsors of these various theories (except for parishioners David and Honan) place any credence in the Senator's testimony. It is because of this wide-spread disbelief that we felt it essential to set down the true, complete story of Chappaquiddick so that the issue will not be diffused by mistaken theories and speculations.

DINIS THE MENACE?

DEPENDING ON HOW YOU LOOK at the Chappaquiddick case, District Attorney Dinis comes off either as a maverick, a fall-guy or a Kennedy agent. His on-again-off-again performance is completely puzzling unless you are willing to accept, without question, the "answer" of politics. How do you view a man who had been both a political ally and opponent of Senator Kennedy?

When the case first broke, Dinis wanted no part of it. He had been up against the Kennedys once, and wanted this case left entirely in the hands of Prosecutor Steele in Edgartown. When the Chappaquiddick affair became a national issue, Dinis immediately jumped in with both feet, demanding inquests and an autopsy. He took the fight to the courts of Pennsylvania yelling foul on the methods used by the Kennedy forces to get Mary Jo's body out of Massachusetts and into a Pennsylvania grave. He was swinging wildly but hard in every direction in his efforts to get an autopsy.

Dinis was really trying in Pennsylvania. However, he learned the power he was up against when Dr. Nevin, without informing him, officially withdrew his request for an autopsy from the Pennsylvania Court of Common Pleas. Nevin jumped, or was pushed, from Dinis' sinking ship. This move had to show Dinis that he was on his own and out of step with the party line.

By the January 1970 inquest, Dinis was a changed man. Whether it was from backroom pressures or having seen the light is speculative, but he seemingly cowered in his corner. Sure he was present and asking questions, but he was no legal ball of fire. Dinis was no menace to anyone, his heart wasn't in it. He had met the enemy and hauled down the flag of justice.

Dinis told reporters that he would vote for Kennedy in the fall senatorial elections—perhaps because they were both on the same Democratic ticket.

With the Grand Jury, the last legal go-round, Dinis was not only disinterested, but some of the jurors said he tried to discourage their efforts and refused to help them. "He did not want us to look into the case," said one jury member. "He was adamant against prosecution. Without his assistance, we were helpless."[1] This was certainly a different Dinis from the one who in 1967 obtained the conviction of a mother who refused to seek medical help for her sick child on religious grounds.[2]

When the Grand Jury quit and announced no indictments to Judge Pacquet, Dinis was quite happy and relieved. He said the case was closed and all investigation into the death of Mary Jo had ended.

This book gives Dinis credit for trying in Pennsylvania but others have indicated that he was on the Kennedy side throughout. Burton Hersh, the Kennedy biographer, says that Dinis requested the inquest in the case as a means of actually brushing the matter under the rug.[3] This would save the Senator from any further unpleasant notoriety. Kennedy could then claim that he had encouraged justice to run its course, and it had vindicated him. Others have been even less kind to Dinis.

Again, the truth is shrouded behind lies, deceptions and smoke screens. If Dinis was really trying, then there is no meaner trick than accusing him of dogging it.

[1] *Human Events*, April 25, 1970.
[2] *Human Events*, January 10, 1970.
[3] Burton Hersh, *The Education of Edward Kennedy*, p. 425.

THE BOILER ROOM GIRLS

THE "BOILER ROOM" GIRLS are the little distractors throughout the whole Chappaquiddick case. This distaff brigade of loyal helpers are the only ones who really played their parts well. They show up better than the men, and win the supporting cast award in their faithful efforts to prop up a terribly weak performance by Sir Teddy.

These girls were old friends with the common background of having worked for Robert Kennedy in his Washington, D.C. boiler room. This was where the running count of convention delegates was kept while RFK was making his play for the presidency. This effort died with RFK when he was assassinated in Los Angeles by Sirhan Sirhan, but the devotion of the girls to the Kennedys and their causes remained. Teddy has always been viewed as the last hope.

The girls had gone on to other jobs but did get together from time to time with each other and the Senator, his aides and his family. Some of them had been entertained at least once previously at the Cape.

These girls were at the cottage that night:

Rosemary "Cricket" Keough, 23 year old college graduate from a wealthy family; she had worked for the Kennedys and their interests since being a JFK volunteer back in high school; she was an indefatigable worker and well liked.

Mary Jo Kopechne, 28 years old; a quiet, attractive career girl who was well thought of; a devotee of politics and a long time Kennedy worshipper.

Maryellen Lyons, at 27 had worked six years for the Kennedys; another college graduate devoted to politics to make a better world and to the Kennedys to implement the politics.

Nance Lyons, 26 and Maryellen's sister; smart, hard working, and equally devoted to the same interests.

Esther Newburgh, 26; an able, attractive career girl; politically liberal and a two year Kennedyite.

Susan Tannenbaum, 24; college graduate, smart and quite liberal, she had hooked on with Robert Kennedy's movement quite naturally.

These girls did not question their part in helping the Senator. Their belief has been that the end justifies the means—that saving Teddy's presidential chances was more important than the truth. What was done was done . . . who was dead was dead . . . and who wanted to be President might still be President if they held the line.

Though they told some conflicting stories after the accident which did not fit the Senator's version, once they learned the Kennedy line they stuck to it. After many months of practice, they put on a flawless performance at the inquest. They have stonewalled what happened, and will sit on that wall till it tumbles down on all their king's men—even though they have been offered over $50,000 each to tell what really happened, to several publications.

There have been reports that the Nixon plumbers tapped their phones and tried to wine and dine information out of them. Evidently neither the big ears nor the beefcakes were able to find out very much. The only press rumor attributable to the plumbers is that the girls were told by the Kennedy forces that they would have no future job worries and would be well taken care of if they held the Kennedy line for at least a certain number of years. The unspoken contrary was that they would have ruined reputations, if not worse.

No matter if they have remained silent only out of loyalty to Teddy, the fact remains that the girls have still not told what really happened that night—the courts know it, the press knows it and the public is slowly becoming aware. If there was a deal struck, the girls know that the Senator had better stick to it, or they could take any future campaign platform apart plank by plank until they have enough wood to rebuild Dyke Bridge.

Jack Anderson says:

From the few remarks the girls have dropped in their private circles, it is clear they don't intend to say anything that would contradict the Senator's story. They belong to a special breed that no politician can be without—bright, efficient, dedicated, hard-working and close-mouthed.

They are tough in the deceptive manner of moss covered hickory, and they possess the singular ability to witness the dirt of the backroom politics and smother it under a blanket of idealism. [1]

Regardless of whether the silence of the boiler room girls was a result of idealism or part of a coverup, it prevented them from telling the truth to Mary Jo's parents. All they were told was the Kennedy line. Mrs. Kopechne doubts that the girls have leveled with her. "I guess those girls just aren't going to talk. It would ease the heartache so much if they would give us some answers."[2]

The girls could have developed a Mary Jo complex where her reputation became their reputation, but it must have worn off by now. The shock of the event is over; only the nagging of their consciences remains.

In the long run, and from the viewpoint of faith to one's clan, such loyalty and devotion—even if misplaced—must be admired. It is far easier to criticize their actions than to find such people ready to walk the final mile for you. This is a breath of fresh air in an otherwise shabby masculine performance. If Mr. Nixon had had some boiler room girls instead of the Deans, Hunts, and Magruders, would he still be in the White House?

[1] Jack Anderson, *"Washington Merry-Go-Round,"* September 2, 1969.
[2] Jack Anderson, *"Washington Merry-Go-Round,"* September 26, 1969.

THE NO-FAULT INSURANCE PAYOFF

EVERYTHING ABOUT THE CHAPPAQUIDDICK CASE has been shrouded in secrecy and deception. It has been a marvelous spawning ground for rumors of all sorts. From the day of the accident, there have been reports that the Kopechnes were well paid for their silence and their fight to block the autopsy. It has been called everything from an insurance settlement to an outright bribe.

The Kennedy forces denied without exception all the claims and speculations, whenever they bothered to take cognizance of them. His aides and friends acted outraged and offended that someone would actually think that Senator Kennedy was part of any such transaction.

Actually, it was only a matter of time. Money doesn't talk, but it sure drops hints. Mary Jo's parents were indeed to be paid. The only question was when, how and the amount to be paid. In the same monotonous fashion everything else in this case had been handled, the Kennedy payment to the Kopechnes was conducted in secrecy and with profuse denials and many outright lies.

By early November, 1974, this part of the story began to unfold. An Associated Press release stated that attorney Joseph Flanagan, who had represented the Kopechnes, announced they had received $140,923 in settlement from Senator Kennedy's insurance company. He stressed that no part of this had been paid by the Senator, and that the sum had been computed on an actuarial basis of expected earnings from Mary Jo if she had lived.

However, like the Senator's first statement to the police, this was not quite the truth. On November 10, 1974, there was a further news report which stated that Senator Kennedy had, in fact, paid over $90,000 of his own money as the insurance company claimed their liability was only $50,000 under Massachusetts law.

Flanagan seemed to be caught in an untruth, perhaps part of a scheme to launder the Senator's money and participation. To set the record straight, Flanagan came up with a whole new story in perfect Chappaquiddick form. This time he bailed himself out by saying that it was part of the settlement agreement that the amount paid by the Senator would be *kept secret*. Like an illegal campaign contribution, the transaction was handled to keep the Senator from being involved. He gave the insurance company his check for $90,000 so the company could give the Kopechnes one check for the full amount. Senator Kennedy was to appear unaware of the entire transaction, and the public would never know the difference.

Since his shock had long passed, the Senator jumped in to kick the ball towards his goal. He had his office say that this was a perfectly natural way to handle the matter—like the quiet way he paid out over $30,000 in legal fees for the ten party goers who remained faithful.

Flashback to 1970 and 1971. Everything about the Kopechnes receiving money was vehemently denied. Now, move up to 1972 when Senator Kennedy was asked how much was paid to the Kopechnes. In a familiar answer he used throughout this case, he said his memory was hazy. The Senator said that since the insurance company had done all the paying, that reporters should ask the Kopechne attorneys—Flanagan *et al.* This must not have been part of the agreement, because when Flanagan was dropped the "hot potato" and told what Kennedy had said, the attorney became very angry, refusing to discuss the matter at all, thereby maintaining his part of the deal, keeping Kennedy's involvement secret.

It all seems to land back at the beginning on Dyke Bridge—who do you believe? Just think about all the conflicts, denials, admissions and lies that have been handed out from time to time by all parties and their attorneys. Think about the way the Edgartown authorities handled the case, and the false "official information" fed to the press, apparently in accordance with a secret settlement agreement.

Whom do you believe and what do you believe? Did Senator Kennedy pay out as much as a half million dollars as rumored? Did he also buy the Kopechnes that second home they suddenly acquired in the Poconos Mountains in Pennsylvania that cost $75,000 — $100,000? Were there other secret settlement agreements? Was it agreed that they would tell the public that the settlement was $140,923 of which the Senator paid two-thirds, when in fact the settlement was half a million dollars and the Senator paid it all? Was temporary silence golden for the Kopechnes? At this point you are forced to take sides and inevitably say you don't believe any of them.

Perhaps with the facts slowly crashing down on Senator Kennedy, the truth will come out. The Kopechnes, now that they have their money, are starting to criticize the Senator and his shock story. They have even said that if Senator Kennedy had reported the accident immediately, their daughter might still be alive. Is this part of a plan, or have the many Chappaquiddick contradictions finally awakened them? We can only hope that the Kopechnes had no part of any coverup, that they are beginning to realize the loss of their daughter can never be compensated and that the truth must come out. It is ironic that they now want the facts made public after they helped the Senator block the autopsy and the answers it would have provided.

THE PRESS IS STARTING TO PRESS

VERY FEW PEOPLE IN PUBLIC LIFE have received the understanding, the consideration and the gentle touch that the press has accorded over the years to the Kennedy brothers. None come to mind offhand. Certainly the Roosevelts never had it so good. Even Eleanor was kicked around regularly. Rockefeller has taken his lumps and McGovern was autopsied daily during 1972.

The Kennedys have been a different story, because the three brothers were all media oriented. The press ignored the bad, looked the other way on the unpleasant and omitted the unfavorable. As the fair-haired boys, the Kennedys could do no wrong. For years the press sugared up, slanted or suppressed many not very nice facts about the Camelot boys.

If you forget John's skirt-chasing and Bobbie's vindictiveness to Hoffa and others, the press did not have too much more to do in glossing over personal foibles in their cases. Neither John nor Bobbie let liquor blur their goals.

With Teddy, there has always been a little more ground to cover up. He has required more inattention than his brothers. The Senator has given the press many opportunities to exercise restraint, because he seems overly fond of the three W's—wine, women and wild driving.

Chappaquiddick may have marked the turning point in the Kennedy press relations. The press has taken a real licking here. They have been conned, used, lied to, refused and pushed around generally. When they couldn't believe that a Kennedy was treating them this way and went back for more, they got it. Between the accident and the TV address, the Senator and his advisors shut them away without even tidbits of information. After the TV address, the Senator announced the matter closed and nothing more would be said. The press investment in being good to Teddy over the years had come up snake eyes.

The television speech itself, where the Senator said he was "free" to tell all, rubbed the salt of insult into press wounds. It told nothing and was offensive to even the moderately intelligent. Not even the two bastions of doctrinaire liberalism—the *Washington Post* and *The New York Times*—could accept it.

Nicholas Von Hoffman of the *Washington Post*, a liberal's liberal, said that the TV address required "work and concentration to believe it." The *Post* itself editorially announced dissatisfaction with the speech.

James Reston of *The New York Times* noted that Kennedy ducked the main questions, evaded the press and avoided cross-examination in court. To say that about a Kennedy was pretty strong stuff for Reston and the *Times*.

Time magazine said he answered a few questions (which?) but raised some new ones and left the most important unanswered. *Life* magazine announced its complete and critical dissatisfaction with Kennedy's sham and fakery.

Jack Anderson, who says he is fond of the Senator personally, but has no friends that block scoops or deadlines, has given the Senator a hard time. In some of the best early reporting on Chappaquiddick, Anderson has specifically said the Senator was not telling the truth on his claims.

After the TV address, Kennedy treated the issue as closed. Later, his forces would bury the autopsy efforts and ignore the inquest proceedings. All the Kennedy attorneys— including those he chose to represent the Kopechnes and partygoers—were doing their best to protect the Senator and keep the facts covered up. Every legal means was used to delay, defeat and avoid further actions. Whatever they couldn't avoid they wanted kept secret. The press protested, but continued to receive pretty short returns for its years of kindness to Ted. Perhaps they had forgotten the saying: Put not thy faith in the gratitude of princes.

The order restricting the inquest and its transcript of proceedings was signed, sealed and delivered to the Kennedy side by the Supreme Court of Massachusetts with everything to be absolutely secret from everybody, maybe for years. In January of 1970, the inquest was held in complete secrecy and the proceedings sealed. In the spring, the grand jury rode up the hill and rode right down again. Still, there was nothing from Kennedy for the press but the back of his hand.

After the grand jury gave up the ghost, and all threat of prosecution was over, the Massachusetts courts decided it was safe to release the inquest transcript. The contents show it could have been released the day of the accident. Everyone had followed the Kennedy line after six months of coaching. The press had been booted down without a real fight.

Chappaquiddick gradually faded away, although two books were written about it. Then came Watergate to keep the press occupied fulltime for a couple of years. They conducted a fierce, never-relenting crusade, which many called a vendetta, until the facts came out. The press ripped bare the whole sorry Watergate scheme, pushed Nixon from office, and forced the prosecution of high ranking officers. With all this accomplished, Chappaquiddick suddenly became newsworthy again.

Human Events, Robert Sherrill, *Time* magazine and the *Boston Globe* all started uncovering the shallow grave of Chappaquiddick during the second half of 1974, especially after the Nixon resignation. Through it all, Kennedy tried to hold his ground.

In September, Kennedy was introduced by one union leader as "the next president of the United States" to an enthusiastic audience. Kennedy announced that if he decided to seek the presidency in 1976, that he would have "a good chance to win the nomination and a reasonable chance to win the election".[1]

It was then that the Press really began to press. Kennedy's 1976 announcement seeking an early honeymoon failed. Two weeks after he threw his driver's license into the presidential ring, he made a "firm, final and unconditional" decision not to seek the presidency in 1976. *Time* magazine said, ". . . Chappaquiddick . . . was probably the chief reason why Kennedy

[1] *The Atlanta Constitution,* September 16, 1974.

withdrew . . . the fact that several publications had renewed investigations into Chappaquiddick may well have affected the timing of Kennedy's announcement."[1]

Such a quick reversal by Kennedy and the revived investigation by the press seemed strange to many. What was the press strategy in reopening what seemed to be a dead issue? Was it self-defense because the public demanded for five years that the truth be told? Was it a carry-over and continuation of the Watergate crusade by a press which hadn't realized its own strength? Was it a press with a guilty conscience realizing they could not allow Democrat Kennedy to continue to enjoy immunity after what had been done to Republican Nixon? Or was the press, without any conscience, trying to show the public it was fair to all?

Many people believe it involves something deeper and more devious. They feel the press was saying something like, "This is just 1974; let's beat this Chappaquiddick thing to death until the public is sick of it. Then by '76 (or '80) Chappie will be old stuff and Teddy will be the candidate." This could really be of serious concern, because Robert Sherrill notes that Kennedy and his aides view the Chappaquiddick matter as being merely a public relations problem.[2]

Perhaps it was not quite so devious and more a matter of strategy. Maybe the press was saying, "Let's bear down on Chappaquiddick and clear it up, once and for all. Get out all the facts and make it a kill or cure job for Teddy. Either he survives it and runs in '76 or '80, or he is dead forevermore at the national level."

No matter which direction the press takes, they will always have to bear a heavy burden for the way Chappaquiddick was handled in 1969 and 1970. One percent of the energy spent on the Watergate Crusade would have solved Chappaquiddick then, and an autopsy would have been held. It would make one wonder whether or not the press can indeed be responsible for the "freedom" it has been accorded.

---

[1] *Time*, October 7, 1974.

[2] A liberal New York columnist described *this* book as an "out and out hatchet job" on the Senator although the columnist had neither seen nor read the book . . . it hadn't even been printed at the time.

WATERGATE VERSUS CHAPPAQUIDDICK

NO MATTER WHEN KENNEDY DECIDES TO RUN for the Presidency, Chappaquiddick will always be an issue and used to counterbalance the stigma of Watergate. It's a political fact of life, and rightly so. The only question is whether the Kennedy forces will be able to diffuse the incident into a "love me, trust me" situation.

Kennedy is well aware of the public and press comparisons of the two national scandals. He addressed himself to the issue, and tried his best to remove himself from the tar baby. The *Boston Globe* in the fall of 1974, reported:

> Kennedy said there were no parallels between the Chappaquiddick incident and the Watergate affair.

> Watergate, he said, "was an attempt to corrupt the political processes of our constitutional system and to violate basic constitutional rights and liberties of individuals in a premeditated and deliberate way. The other (Chappaquiddick) was a tragic accident.

> "Secondly, on the one hand, I have been willing to accept complete responsibility. I have described my conduct, in a way which I don't think any public official has ever described his conduct at any time in the history that I have read about, as being indefensible, about being irrational, about being—and on the other hand, you have an individual who has refused to accept any real responsibility for that action, has refused to appear before court as I did, and refused to accept the penalty of guilt, which I did.

> "Thirdly, the people that were involved in the Chappaquiddick incident were bystanders and innocent. And only had for

the most part, casual knowledge of the accident to themselves and who are not witnesses. On the other hand, in the Watergate, you had only those that were involved with the planning and the scheming of the destruction of evidence and the misleading of congressional committees.

"And on the other hand, you had those individuals that appeared voluntarily and responded to each and every one of their questions that were put to them."

Many wonder if Senator Kennedy actually said all that with a straight face. Even from his Mt. Olympus the parallels should be obvious to the wily politician from Hyannis Port.

First of all, even though Kennedy said there were "no" parallels between Chappaquiddick and Watergate, the reader of this book will know there are many. Both attempted to "corrupt" our system in a "deliberate way". The real difference is that the whole sordid Watergate story has come out, the guilty removed from office and many put in prison, while Kennedy and those giving contradictory testimony have never been punished. The corruption of the legal system in Massachusetts and Pennsylvania is lasting, because it has not been ferreted out by the press and straightened out by the courts. Watergate was broken down the middle, Chappaquiddick has been locked away for protection. Both symbolize corruption.

Kennedy said, "I have been willing to accept complete responsibility", but only for his version of what happened. As we have shown, what he said happened and what *did* happen are worlds apart. His efforts to block the truth show that he is not willing to accept complete responsibility.

Kennedy said he has accepted the penalty of guilt, but only to the crime of leaving the scene of an accident—which many say does not really relate to what occurred. When Judge Boyle mildly criticized the Senator and doubted his truthfulness, Kennedy lashed back, ". . . the inference and ultimate finding of the judge's report are not justified and I reject them." That was quite a Jovian statement by a man who is "willing to accept complete responsibility".

The Chappaquiddick case goes beyond one man—the actions of Gargan, Markham, partygoers and Edgartown officials are all interwoven. Though the Senator said these people were innocent bystanders who had only "casual knowledge", this is quite an understatement. The police knew about his 17 calls when he was supposedly in shock—is that casual knowledge or were they "involved with the planning and the scheming of the destruction and concealment of evidence". It is not even necessary to mention the lack of any investigation nor how conveniently there was never a standard autopsy performed.

Gargan and Markham helped obtain a boat for Kennedy, which goes way beyond casual knowledge into perjury because of the Kennedy swim story. Everyone at the party testified that the Senator and Mary Jo left at about 11:15, yet they were spotted by Look at 12:45. Is that casual knowledge? All the Kennedy party was "involved with the planning and the scheming of the destruction of evidence", because they picked the cottage clean, hid Mary Jo's purse, and got quickly off the island before any questions could be asked. From the day of the accident through the inquest to the present, they have all helped to mislead the courts, the press and the public. None of them has voluntarily come forward to be grilled by the press on the details. No Senate committee will ever hold hearings on this case as were held in the Watergate scandal. Nor has any state or federal bar association instituted any disbarment inquiry against the Senator or his attorneys as was done with Mr. Nixon and his aides.

The comparisons are endless, endless. Kennedy can deny it until he panics again, but the parallels are valid. Two years of Watergate was hard on the soul of the nation, but the truth was known in the end. How many years will our national integrity remain shrouded until Chappaquiddick has a similar conclusion?

CREDIBILITY

THE ENTIRE CHAPPAQUIDDICK CASE hinges upon credibility — whom and what do you believe? This has plagued reporters and investigators since the morning Mary Jo's body was found. The secrecy, denials, falsehoods and cover-up that have prevailed from the beginning have pushed the decision into the Senator's camp—that is, "if you don't believe Senator Kennedy then you're obviously against all the Kennedys and everything they stand for." The first step in confusing the issue to help Teddy has been achieved.

The decision of credibility has nothing to do with the Kennedy legacy of Camelot, myth or fact. It is not a popularity contest or a party vote. In reaching this decision on credibility, some well-settled legal principles can be of assistance. These principles are not only "good" law, but they also constitute sound common sense. You might keep in mind that the Bible says ". . . the guilty flee where no man pursueth." The law agrees because the judge will instruct the jury that *The unexplained, or insufficiently explained, flight from the scene of crime can itself be a factor affecting guilt.*

There is also available an admonition by the judge on considering the interest of the different parties and witnesses as affecting credibility. The judge tells the jury—in this case the reader—that *In weighing the testimony of any witness, you should consider what interest such witness, including the accused, has in the outcome of the case.*

Chappaquiddick is a situation whereby the reporters, reviewers and investigators are virtually unanimous in either flatly disbelieving or having grave doubts about most of the material testimony by or on behalf of Senator Kennedy. Judge Boyle in his inquest report announced specific disbelief of the

Senator in several areas. Let's review some of them:

The claims of moderate drinking as compared to the large amounts of unaccounted for liquor that disappeared.

When did the Senator and Mary Jo leave the party?

What was their destination when they left?

Did the Senator turn into Dyke Road to the beach by mistake?

Was the Senator familiar with Dyke Road?

Does the Senator truly not remember how he got out of the car?

Did the Senator repeatedly dive into the water trying to save Mary Jo?

Did the Senator swim the 500 foot channel back to Edgartown?

Was the Senator in such a state of shock that he didn't fully realize what happened until 9 hours later when he went to the police station?

The foregoing items are not all-inclusive, but they are material, important and have been the subjects of falsehood. To cover this, there is a standard instruction the judge will give the jury. Lawyers refer to the instruction as *falsus in uno, falsus in omnibus*. The jury is instructed that *If you believe any witness has knowingly testified falsely about any material fact, then you are at liberty to disregard that part or* all *of the testimony of such witness.* This is an important point for the reader—who is now a member of the public jury—to remember throughout this whole case. Much of the Senator's testimony rests upon his being in shock and not in his right mind. If this is disproved or you do not believe this, then his whole story is shattered.

Now we come to another and even graver aspect of credibility. There is no question but that throughout the case, Senator Kennedy and his lawyers have used every possible tactic to keep the public and the press from learning the facts about Chappaquiddick. They opposed every action and proceeding—including autopsy, inquest and grand jury—that might have brought out the facts. There is a jury instruction which is actually intended for a less aggravated situation that takes care of this *The jury is instructed that if there is pertinent evidence peculiarly available to one party and such party fails to produce or prevents the production of such evidence, then the jury may infer that such evidence, if produced, would be unfavorable to that party.*

Senator Kennedy is a lawyer, and knows all about these things. His lawyers knew all of these rules when they persisted in putting a tight lid on the evidence. With this in mind, we the public jury are entitled to infer that they determined it was safer to suppress and to be accused of suppressing the truth than to let the truth be known.

PERSONAL OBSERVATIONS

IT IS POSSIBLE that some of the following may be mildly repetitious, but the areas involved have been the subject of deliberate falsification and are crucial. This was written after a thorough personal investigation of the Chappaquiddick and Edgartown areas. The lodging used was the Shiretown Inn where Senator Kennedy and some of his party had stayed. The subjects under consideration are:

    the beach shack
    the mistaken turn
    the sudden bridge
    the moderate speed
    the lost hour
    the invisible light.

The Beach Shack Lawrence Cottage is not a ramshackle little beach picnic affair. It is not a shack a group would shun as suitable overnight quarters. It is a substantial, well-built place, a home for year-round living, and well able to accommodate vacation sleeping arrangements for a dozen people. It looks like a permanent home. It has a well-kept yard. The house is completely surrounded by a well-groomed lawn, fenced in, and in turn surrounded by woods which come up to the yard area. Quite private.

The Mistaken Turn You can never in this world "mistakenly" turn off School Road down Dyke Road to the bridge and the deserted beaches beyond. To go onto Dyke Road you must make a 90 degree turn to the right instead of 90 degrees to the left, an error of 180 degrees. In addition, you go from a smooth, two-lane paved road onto a narrow, rough country dirt road with the trees closing in on you from both sides. The claim of "mistake" just doesn't hold up.

The Sudden Bridge   The bridge over Poucha Pond never jumped out in front of Senator Kennedy or anyone else. The bridge has been there many years without surprising anyone. For over 1,500 feet before the bridge the road is a straightaway, and for the last 500 feet the bridge is clearly visible. To be "surprised" by the bridge you have to be loaded or not looking plus traveling at a high rate of speed. There is just no other way.

The Moderate Speed   Senator Kennedy, Judge Boyle, the prosecutors and the proceedings all refer to moderate speed, careful driving, and a speed of 20 to 22 miles per hour. Without qualification or hesitation we say these statements are false.

The authors have maintained throughout the opinion that the Kennedy car had to be going at least 40 to 50 miles per hour when it went off the bridge. It had to be going that fast for that heavy car to turn a rolling flip, hit the water on its top and right side, smashing in the passenger side windows and coming to rest upsidedown on the bottom of the pond. If the car had been going 20 miles an hour it would have nosed off the bridge landing in an upright position or on its right side on the bottom. After viewing the scene there is no question but that we were right. Some questions were asked and the answers were found. Others have shared our views all along, despite Judge Boyle's reference to "twenty miles per hour" in his inquest findings.

Here is what we were told about the inquest speed situation. The Registry of Motor Vehicles of Massachusetts offered evidence at the inquest to show that the car was going 35 to 40 miles per hour at the time, but Judge Boyle would not accept it. The proceedings were stopped, the parties went off the record, and the Judge stated he would not allow evidence of speed more than 20 or 22 miles per hour. The Registry witness gave evidence on that basis. The Judge not only ruled against evidence of a higher (more truthful) speed but actually had the references to it physically expunged from the record.

The Registry prepared its 35- to 40-mile-per-hour speed case after an exhaustive study of all physical aspects and measurements: skid marks, heights, depths, distances, weight, trajectories, and so forth. These figures are still available if you are interested. See Figure 7 in the compilation *You, The Jury* by R.B. Cutler, 1969, and 1973 (privately printed), and give them to your own expert. Or go take a look at the bridge, picture the accident in your mind, and you won't need an expert. The authors were pleased to obtain this information, though not surprised by it. That kind of speed at that time and place indicates criminal homicide in any state regardless of the later conduct of fleeing the scene and the ensuing results of that action.

The Lost Hour Senator Kennedy places the accident at around 11:30 p.m. on July 18; Sheriff Look's testimony would have it at about 12:45 a.m. on July 19. The time discrepancy is easily disposed of as little credence has been given the claims of the Senator. Conversely, there is not and has never been any doubt about the testimony by Sheriff Look. But let us disregard the sheriff and settle the "lost hour" problem solely on the basis of the sworn testimony by Senator Kennedy and on the cold, irrefutable figures regarding time and the tide at the bridge over Poucha Pond.

The Senator says 11:30 p.m. or so, so be it. The Senator also testified about his efforts to rescue Mary Jo from the sunken car. At the inquest the Senator, under oath, said that as soon as he got out of the car:

"I was swept away by the tide that was flowing at an extraordinary rate through that narrow cut there and was swept along by the tide. . . ."

(The current swept him along) ". . . approximately 30 to 50 feet."

"I would think 30 to 40 feet."

"I couldn't swim back (to the car) at that time because of the current."

And when he dove to save Mary Jo, ". . . the tide would sweep out this way there, and then I dove repeatedly from this side until, I would say the end, and then I was swept away from (it) the first couple of times, again back over to this side."

And in the Senator's famous television "explanation speech" he referred to the "strong and murky current".

At the time (11:30 p.m.) of these heroic efforts against the on-rushing and sweeping waters the tide tables indicate that at that precise time on July 18, 1969, at Poucha Pond, Chappaquiddick the tide was slack, complete low tide, a dead calm, there *was no* current.

However, if Senator Kennedy did in fact make efforts to rescue Mary Jo, and if he should be in error on the time, and if Sheriff Look is correct on the time, then we would have a different picture. At 12:50 to 1:00 a.m. on the nineteenth the tide at Poucha Pond had changed and *was* running hard, three to four knots and getting stronger, working up to its maximum speed of five knots.

The Senator picked his action time and stuck to it. He can have his time, or he can have his sweeping, rushing, extraordinary tide, but he can't have them both.

The Invisible Light   The Senator testified that he did not see "a cottage with a light on it" although it is agreed that the Malm Cottage or Dyke House just before the bridge did have such a light. At night in that area it is pitch black and any light from inside or outside of that house comes on like a beacon. You cannot pass the house without seeing it. It is visible up and down the road and from the bridge.

It is entirely possible that a person almost out of his mind in fear-crazed panic might dash headlong by. But such a person would not have just finished twenty minutes of diving for the body of a friend trapped in a car and another fifteen or twenty minutes resting on the bank before going by. Here again, it cannot be both ways.

But it is possible for one to go by the lighted Dyke House deliberately and quietly if one were in trouble and didn't want to call for help, preferring to have one's friends straighten things out. In any event, such a person and the road would be bathed in a stream of light from the house.

For the sake of argument, consider the six items discussed above as controversial, disputable or contradictory. Don't take anyone's word for what happened. Go to Chappaquiddick and see for yourself. All the facts are there and available.

THE CAUSE OF DEATH

THERE ARE FOUR PROFESSIONALLY SKILLED PERSONS who are qualified to give opinions as to the exact cause of Mary Jo Kopechne's death. One says she drowned, one says her death was consistent with drowning and the other two say death resulted from suffocation.

Captain John N. Farrar, of the Scuba Search and Rescue Division of the Edgartown Fire Department, with almost twenty years experience as a diver, recovered the body of Mary Jo from the sunken car.

Doctor Donald R. Mills, Associate County Medical Examiner, examined the body at the scene after its recovery by Captain Farrar.

Eugene Frieh, mortician, and his assistant, David Guay, were called to the scene by the authorities. They were present during the examination by Dr. Mills, and took the body to Frieh's funeral home where they prepared and embalmed it.

To make a determination of death by drowning with regard to a body fresh out of the water would seem to be a relatively routine diagnosis, but medical experts say otherwise. Doctor Werner Spitz, Deputy Chief Medical Examiner for the State of Maryland, appeared on behalf of the Kopechnes in the Pennsylvania court proceedings where he testified that:

> ... the diagnosis of drowning is one of the hardest diagnoses in forensic pathology, in the fresh body. ...

To reach a correct diagnosis there must be affirmative anatomical findings of conditions that arise from drowning, and negative findings to exclude other possible causes of death. Without such findings,

... it would be as good as impossible for me, and I presume for any experienced forensic pathologist, to make a definitive answer, to give a definitive answer as to whether a person drowned or whether a person asphyxiated, for example, due to lack of air.

Among the tests made are:

Examining for hemorrhages of the inner ear, present in over 70 per cent of the cases.
.The swelling of the lungs because the lungs are large with water and the water will exude on the cut surface.
The presence of diatoms and algae in remote parts of the body.
The presence or absence of foreign material deep in the airway and the bronchi.
Considerable quantities of water in the stomach.
The presence of above average chloride content in the left side of the heart in salt water drownings.
And the various negative findings that death was not caused by any obvious wound or means, or by skull or spinal fracture, rupture of the aorta, or other internal injury.

The above are tests that are made routinely during an autopsy; none, of course, were made in this case. While the aforementioned tests are elementary to those skilled in pathology, the lay person interested in pursuing the subject will find references made to these items in Moenssens, Moses and Inbau, *Scientific Evidence in Criminal Cases*, pp. 179, et seq.; Soderman and O'Connell, *Modern Criminal Investigation*, pp. 283 et seq.; or see any standard text on the subject or check your local Rescue Squad.

Finally, for us "lay people", there is a medically approved universal test. When a person drowns, the body sinks to the bottom. It stays there, according to experts, for two to three, and maybe more days depending on temperature, putrefication rate, and so forth. It then returns to the surface. The important point here is that Mary Jo's body never sank.

Dr. Mills said it was his opinion that Mary Jo's death was a result of drowning. He made his examination about 9:30 a.m., July 19, 1969, at the scene, after the body had been recovered by Captain Farrar. Dr. Mills said death had occurred five to eight hours (nine at the outside) earlier — that is, between 12:30 and 4:30 a.m. At the formal inquest six months later, the doctor changed his opinion and stated death had occurred "six or more hours earlier" (from 3:30 a.m. back) and could not give outside limits.

On July 8, 1975, the authors asked Dr. Mills about the time discrepancy in these statements (it was very beneficial to Senator Kennedy) but he said he felt there was no real conflict. He stated he now had no independent recollection of times but if there was any issue that his original statement at the scene should control.

Further, at the inquest, with literally no evidence, Judge Boyle made a finding of death that moved the time back to as early as 11:30 p.m. the night before.

Dr. Mills testified:

I formed my opinion by the fact that this girl was completely filled with water; that is her bronchial tubes were full, her mouth was full of water. There was water in her nose. This was clearly demonstrated by making just light pressure on the chest wall in which case water would simply pour out of the mouth and nose. There was some foam about the nose and mouth which is characteristic of drowning.

Dr. Mills stated he found no incised wounds or bruises, that he did not find it necessary to remove all clothing, he felt there was no need for an autopsy, and turned the body over to Eugene Frieh, the mortician.

Mr. Frieh appeared at the inquest and was asked what he observed in regard to Dr. Mills' examination. He answered:

A. Well, the usual procedure of general examination of a body so found. Dr. Mills loosened up the front of the blouse, took his stethoscope and applied it to various sections of the thoracic region and the abdominal region. He also manipulated the thoracic region with his hands.

Q. Did this produce a flow of water?

A. And looked at her eyes.

Q. Did this produce a flow of water?

A. It produced some water flow, water and foam, mostly foam.

Mr. Frieh also testified in the Pennsylvania proceedings which attempted to obtain an autopsy. He told of cleaning and preparing the body at his funeral home and was asked:

Q. Did you manipulate the body in any way as to extract water from the body?

A. As is our custom on a drowning case, we usually use what is called a body block. May I go into detail?

Q. Yes.

A. A body block is placed under the abdominal area thereby compressing that area very precisely.

Q. Did you do this?

A. Yes.

Q. What did this produce, if anything?

A. A very little moisture, sir.

Q. Did you find this unusual?

(Objection made and overruled)

A. I did raise an eyebrow, sir, in the sense that I expected much more moisture.

Then in July, 1970, with the anniversary of Chappaquiddick pending, the Boston *Herald American* interviewed Mr. Frieh, who stated he felt that Mary Jo may well have suffocated rather than drowned. Mr. Frieh noted that water ordinarily issues freely and in some quantity from the body of a drowned person, but that no more than a cup of moisture came from the body.[1] He would have testified to this at both hearings, he said, but *no one asked him.*

Frieh indicated Mary Jo may have died from inhaling her own carbon dioxide; the lack of water in her body indicated suffocation rather than drowning. When he and Dr. Mills went to Wilkes-Barre for the hearings in October, 1969, he said he did his best to persuade his friend Dr. Mills to change his finding on the cause of death from drowning to asphyxiation.

David Guay, Frieh's assistant, was present at the scene when the body was recovered and later did much of the preparing and embalming of the body. Originally he had been quoted as agreeing with Frieh, but when we talked to him in October and November of 1975 he said Mary Jo's condition at the scene was consistent with drowning although he later obtained only 8 to 10 ounces of water from the body.

Frieh told the authors he would not discuss the case with anyone, though he conceded that only a very small quantity of water came from the body. Other than that he referred us to his court testimony. Frieh claimed he would not talk because he had been misquoted by a reporter but refused to name the reporter, the paper, the interview or the claimed erroneous quote. Our feeling was strong that someone had been giving him a hard time for talking about the case. We were later told that Mr. Frieh had claimed his earlier discussions had cost him $10,000 in lost business, but he did not claim that he had been misquoted in any way. To his intimates, Mr. Frieh's position on the facts of the case remains unchanged.

Captain John Farrar of the Edgartown Rescue Squad has been adamant throughout that Mary Jo's life might have been saved if he had been called earlier. He feels very strongly about the case. With regard to Mary Jo staying alive in the car for some time, he was prepared to testify about the large quantities of air still in the car ten or eleven hours after the accident when the car was being salvaged. He stated that Judge Boyle would not allow him to give this evidence and that

---

[1] This may have been swallowed during the car's plunge into the water before Mary Jo positioned herself in the air pocket where found.

Judge Boyle later ruled in his report that ". . . there is no evidence that any air remained in the immersed car".

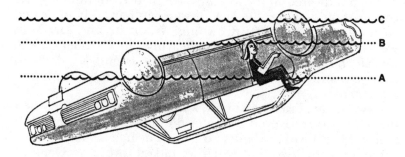

A. Captain Farrar believes this would be the original level of the water held there by the trapped air as the car settled.

B. Captain Farrar's estimate of the final water level inside the car and the trunk.

C. Pond water level.

Captain Farrar testified in both court proceedings and has given lectures that related the position of the body (see illustration) when he found it: neck stretched, head bent back seeking the last bit of air, the gritted teeth, the wedged legs, the raised arms, and the hands and fingers bent into talons clutching the seat edge, all evidence of the tremendous but futile efforts made by Mary Jo to survive.

Captain Farrar waxes vehement while speaking of a "teacup of water" found in a "drowned" body when the water in drowned persons is measured in quarts and gallons. He explains that when a person drowns the body sinks, but says that wasn't the case here. The body when found was in a semiupright position in the uppermost part of the car, not in the lower part where a drowned person would have been found. Captain Farrar says the body had never lost its buoyancy, that when he took it out of the car it virtually floated up to the surface. "Oh, Mary Jo drowned all right," stated the Captain, "she drowned in her own carbon dioxide."

Dr. Mills adheres to his opinion of death by drowning but wishes there had been an autopsy, pointing out that the final decision of "no autopsy" emanated from the District Attorney's Office. He testified in the Pennsylvania proceedings that he later recommended an autopsy to the District Attorney's Office due to the circumstances of the unwitnessed accident and the prominence of the people involved.

Apparently all of the other doctors agree that there should have been an autopsy, their views ranging from desirable and proper to mandatory. Medical authorities in general and Massachusetts regulations in particular would require an autopsy. The doctors and medical authorities all seem to hold that in making "one of the hardest diagnoses in forensic pathology" on the basis of the "exam" by Dr. Mills, it would be "impossible . . . for any experienced forensic pathologist" to determine whether this death was caused by suffocation or drowning.

So there it is. Four persons who are involved in this case are fully qualified to comment on the possible cause of death, based on actual facts. Two of them insist it was due to suffocation. One says it was by drowning, one says consistent with drowning. To reach drowning you must ignore the fact that the "drowned" body didn't sink. If it didn't sink, it didn't drown.

The authors believe it is clear that Mary Jo consciously took the position in the uppermost portion of the car to take advantage of the air trapped in that "top" portion, that she positioned herself and propped her arms and legs and gripped her hands in an effort to hold herself there. She remained in this position for a substantial period of time (perhaps for as long as three or four hours, according to medical testimony). She died in this position after exhausting the oxygen in the trapped air pocket. *Rigor mortis* set in while the body remained in the tense position taken before death. The bent, stiff body with gritted teeth and clawed hands was found in that position and remained so bent when taken to the surface and examined by Dr. Mills.

The precise sequence of events were known only to Kennedy and Mary Jo, but it is presumed from the evidence that after Kennedy escaped the car settled into the silt, wedging the doors and preventing free egress through the windows. The terror-stricken girl did not have the strength to force her way out of the vehicle, but had enough presence of mind to seek the air pocket, waiting for her companion to free her from what became her watery tomb.

This then is the real horror of the case, Mary Jo in the bottom of that upside-down car, wedged in, clawing, clutching and straining for air and for life in the total blackness at the bottom of Poucha Pond with the water creeping higher and higher. Completely terrified, she waited for help from Senator Kennedy — who was on the phone seeking help not for Mary Jo, but for Senator Kennedy.

A little more horror? Some of his phone calls made before reporting the matter to the police, dealt with the possibilities of getting the "body" off the Island and out of the jurisdiction. The sad fact is that these discussions were perhaps premature in the sense that the "body" was not yet in fact a "body".

Part Four

Panic For President?

PANIC FOR PRESIDENT?

THE AFTERMATH OF THE CHAPPAQUIDDICK TRAGEDY and cover-up has had some positive results. Teddy Kennedy's presidential ambitions will no longer be peddled to the American people on the basis of the previous Kennedys' legacies. If anything, the comparison of Teddy to his two brothers and the myth that surrounds those two will be a detrimental one. The memories of Jack and Bobby are very dear to many people, and Teddy has besmirched that revered name.

In a convention deadlock or the more likely possibility of an absolute wasteland of Democratic candidates, the Kennedy name will be his ace. It will be a tarnished advantage, with Chappaquiddick only a public relations problem in the eyes of the Kennedy team.

For the next several national election years, Chappaquiddick will be thin ice for the Senator. Teddy has felt the heat and may soon touch the fire. The memory of Mary Jo brought a quick backlash to the Senator's seemingly self-incriminating proclamation: "Do we operate under a system of equal justice under the law? Or is there one system for the average citizen and another for the high and mighty?" Though he was talking about the Nixon pardon, it almost seemed a cruel joke upon the public and the legal system that he and his forces so successfully immobilized.

In a belated investigation of their home-state Senator, the friendly *Boston Globe*, in the Fall of 1974, concluded that:

Inept prosecution and preferential treatment of . . . Kennedy by law enforcement and judicial officials probing the death of

Mary Jo Kopechne apparently saved Sen. Kennedy from being charged with serious driving crimes, including manslaughter.

Routine investigative and judicial procedure was either altered or botched numerous times to Sen. Kennedy's benefit during the three official probes of the accident—the initial police investigation, the inquest and the grand jury sessions.

The investigative failings appear to have resulted from an overwhelming deference to Kennedy's power and prestige by apprehensive officials. . . .

The *Globe's* investigation seemed sensational, because it is a leading Massachusetts paper. Their analysis was good, but they weren't out to bring him down in the manner that the *Washington Post* went after and finally got Nixon.

Even though the *Globe* had fired on Kennedy with blanks and paper wads, Kennedy lashed back, stating emotionally, "These charges are ugly, untrue and grossly unfair." He went on to say:

It is regrettable, in the atmosphere of doubt and suspicion which enshrouds us as a people, that the truth cannot compete with the unnamed sources, the groundless suggestions and the speculations which are nurtured by articles of sensationalism.

The main problem the truth has had all along is competing with the Kennedy power and money. The doubts and suspicions are a natural byproduct of its coverup.

What is strange about his response is that Kennedy voluntarily reopened much of the 1974 flashback on Chappaquiddick. He first disavowed any Presidential ambitions and then held a *Globe* interview so lengthy it had to be serialized. Was Senator Kennedy trying to cloud the issue, or was he testing the water at Poucha Pond to see what facts the investigative reporters had, and whether any of the party goers would break down to immense financial offers?

Perhaps Kennedy was trying to exhaust the whole subject so that by 1976 or 1980 the Democrats would "force" him to run for the good of the country (that is, the Party). With a string of losers from 1968 on, the Democrats are getting hungry for a return to power. Kennedy, with the hindsight of what Nixon should have done about Watergate in early 1972, can see history in the re-making.

James Reston said, "Kennedy seems to believe that he could have survived (the '72 primaries), won the nomination, lost ten points on Chappaquiddick and picked up twenty on Watergate," winning the Presidency of a divided country.[1]

Senator Kennedy may still have his options open. Boston Mayor Kevin White said Kennedy "may change his mind and accept the presidential nomination (because) the American public is hungry for strong leadership."[2] So much for the Sherman statement.

One of the lasting effects of Chappaquiddick will be on Kennedy's credibility. Whether in the Senate or in the White House, Kennedy can never again be really effective. He could have easily lived down another drinking scandal, but the memory of Mary Jo left under water for nine hours will never leave the nation. It will continue to haunt his Senate debates and public speeches. In a heated vote or a political crusade, people will always blur his appearance with the vision of Mary Jo gasping for breath. His judgement will always be in question.

Did Chappaquiddick change Senator Kennedy into a more mature man? James Reston said, ". . . the irony is that, by the accident, he was startled into both maturity and responsibility. . . ."[3] However, Arthur Egan—the journalist who broke the story of the 17 phone calls—reported in the *New Hampshire Sunday News* in 1972:

> Two high-stepping playboy U.S. Senators, taking advantage of a Congressional recess, spent a pre-Labor Day holiday sailing around Penobscot Bay with two lovely females who were definitely not their wives.
>
> Senators Edward M. Kennedy and John V. Tunney spent at least four days aboard the Curragh, Kennedy's power sloop, with the two women.

[1] James Reston, *San Antonio Express*, September 27, 1974.
[2] *Atlanta Journal*, December 3, 1974.
[3] James Reston, *San Antonio Express*, September 27, 1974.

One of the women with the Senators has been identified as Mrs. Amanda Burden, the pretty 26-year-old wife of Carter Burden, New York millionaire socialite and Democratic councilman.

Both *Newsweek* and the *Washington Post* linked Kennedy and Mrs. Burden romantically. She has since divorced her husband, and Tunney's marriage went on the rocks. Has Teddy really matured, or is he just plain lacking in common sense?

No matter what else Chappaquiddick has proven about Senator Kennedy, it has raised serious questions of whether he is qualified to be President of the United States. His own words and conduct in his time of crisis must be considered in this regard.

In his police statement the morning after the accident, the Senator said:

> I was exhausted and in a state of shock. . . .I remember. walking around for a period of time and then going back to my hotel room. . . . When I fully realized what had happened this morning [after 10 hours] I immediately notified the police.

Can you imagine what might have happened if F.D.R. had acted in a similar fashion when Pearl Harbor was bombed? In his television speech, the Senator admitted:

> My conduct and conversations during the next several hours [after the accident], to the extent that I can remember them, make no sense to me at all . . . (My thoughts were) scrambled . . . confused . . . irrational . . . (and I said and did) inexplicable, inconsistent and inconclusive things . . . I was overcome, I'm frank to say, by a jumble of emotions: grief, fear, doubt, exhaustion, *panic*, confusion and shock. (Emphasis added.)

If Lincoln had been overcome by such irrational thoughts after Bull Run, would Dixie be our national anthem? If LBJ had gone into shock during the 1967 Middle Eastern War, would the Russians have made Israel just a memory?

Each of Kennedy's statements has him reporting to the police "immediately"—as soon as his mental confusion and panic had cleared and he realized what had happened nine to ten hours earlier. Could a President of the United States function in a time of crisis with such reactions? Could the United States afford to wait for such a President to react? Would the world wait? The finger on the nuclear trigger bears awesome burdens.

Can Senator Kennedy handle the responsibility of the Presidency? In 1972, a worried nation forced the removal of Senator Eagleton from McGovern's ticket because of what could have happened were he to become President. If Teddy had been in Jack's place during the Cuban missile crisis, the history of the world—if one still existed—might be far different.

Part Five

Questions With Answers

QUESTIONS WITH ANSWERS

NO CONTEMPORARY CASE has given rise to more discussion, argument and unanswered questions as Chappaquiddick. There are three basic reasons for this: (1) Senator Kennedy's refusal to truthfully discuss the case; (2) The contrived silence of all the party participants; and (3) The gross failure of the authorities to properly investigate and prosecute the case.

The following 43 questions (with answers for a change) were gathered from:

"20 Questions," *Human Events* Special Supplement, November 2, 1974.
"Special Report—27 Questions," Republican National Committee.
The questions raised in the 1974 *Boston Globe* investigation.
Robert Sherrill's article, "Chappaquiddick + 5."
Jack Anderson's columns and other media articles.

The questions are paraphrased from the above sources, and the answers are the result of the authors' extensive investigation. The answering of these questions is within the power of Senator Kennedy who is merely delaying the inevitable.

1. When did Kennedy (and Mary Jo) leave the cottage?
Probably for the last time about 12:30 a.m. He later pushed his schedule back an hour, otherwise he could not claim they were going to catch the ferry that stopped at midnight. If he in fact left around 11:15 p.m., then he and Mary Jo had an hour in which they could have acquired the "blood stain" on her blouse before being seen at Dyke Road by Sheriff Look.

2. Was Kennedy headed for the ferry?

No, he was headed for the secluded beach.

3. Did Mary Jo think they were going back to Edgartown?
No, that is why she didn't take her purse.

4. How could Kennedy turn into Dyke Road without realizing his mistake?
It was no mistake.

5. If Deputy Sheriff Look saw the Senator and Mary Jo at 12:45 a.m., what about the period from 11:15 p.m. (when they supposedly left the cottage) until then?
In the absence of a better explanation from the Senator, and if they did leave the cottage at the time claimed, then this "lost hour" might account for the grass stains on the back of Mary Jo's blouse.

6. Did Senator Kennedy see Sheriff Look?
Yes, and he took off quickly to avoid contact with the law.

7. How dangerous is the bridge and its approach?
Reasonable care and attention will keep you dry. No one else has gone off Dyke Bridge in 25 years at the time of this writing.

8. How fast was Kennedy driving as he approached the bridge?
The experts, unnecessarily restricted by Judge Boyle, said 20-22 mph. Other investigators, unrestricted, believe the car was going substantially faster considering the physical evidence, including the fact the car went 34 feet after leaving the bridge. The driving habits of the Senator in the past tend to support the latter view. We think he was going 40-50 mph.

9. How could Kennedy escape from the car?
His window was upright and open like an escape hatch when the car landed on the passenger side (mostly) blowing out those windows, and the water poured in those windows as the car slowly turned turtle and sank to the bottom; the driver's window remaining open for an appreciable time.

10. Why couldn't Mary Jo get out?
The blown out windows on her side were the inflow avenue for the rushing water, and were pointed towards the bottom of the pond. These windows were under water the entire time from when the car hit until it settled on the bottom of the pond. She was barred from escape by the window on the driver's side (until too late) by Senator Kennedy who was above and on top of her while he got out of that window.

11. In the Senator's condition, how could he dive repeatedly for Mary Jo?
He didn't.

12. Why didn't Kennedy immediately call for help?
Panic! He told the truth when he kept mentioning "panic" in his various statements. Markham said Kennedy told him that after he got out of the car, *"He tried to go back into the water again to see if he could get Miss Kopechne or try to open the door or something. He said he couldn't.* He said the only thing he could think of was to come back and get us (Gargan and Markham) to see if we could help."

13. Why didn't the Senator seek help from the lighted houses or the fire station he passed on the way back to the cottage?
Panic, and, as he said later to Markham, he could only think of getting back to the cottage to Markham and Gargan for help.

14. Did Gargan and Markham try to rescue Mary Jo?
Neither Kennedy nor Markham or Gargan tried to rescue her. The best evidence indicates their "rescue" effort was fabricated, at least in part, to answer the criticism—and possible charges—for their failure to report the accident. The Senator made no mention of these heroics in his first confession to the police the morning of the accident.

15. Why didn't Markham and Gargan, who were both lawyers, call for help?
Possibly they were intoxicated and/or were also in a panic. Kennedy is their leader, and could have dominated them into

doing nothing on the theory that it was too late and they needed the time to come up with a good story or alibi for the Senator to save his political future.

16.   Could Mary Jo have been saved?
Prompt action probably would have saved her according to John Farrar, the diver who recovered the body, and other experts. Mary Jo's position when found, was with her head thrust up into an "air pocket" and her hands still hooked like talons, holding herself in position. According to the statement by Dr. Mills as to the time of death after examining the body at the accident scene, it was indicated that she could have lived from one to three hours after the accident.

17.   In his condition, how could Kennedy swim back to Edgartown?
He didn't. After his experience in the car at Poucha Pond, wild horses couldn't have gotten him back in that water.

18.   Since the Senator changed clothes and seemed normal at the Shiretown Inn at 2:25 a.m., was he still in shock as claimed?
We have no argument with any claim of original shock and panic at the time of the accident, but thereafter, the shock seems to be selective as needed, and false.

19.   How could any man (the Senator), calmly chat with Ross Richards on Saturday morning about sailing, while his friend (Mary Jo) was still at the bottom of Poucha Pond?
If you really want this one answered, ask Senator Kennedy.

20.   How could the Senator's shock be so selective that he could call his aides but not the police?
It wasn't but he did.

21.   What was Kennedy doing on Chappaquiddick at 9:30 the next morning?
Apparently still wondering and undecided—and probably afraid—as to exactly what course should be taken. He and his aides made at least 17 long distance phone calls during the night, trying to plan for or possibly delay the moment of truth.

22. Why did Kennedy wait 9-10 hours to report the accident?
Panic and the inability to face his crisis.

23. Since it was known that a famous politician was involved in the death, why did not Doctor Mills automatically order an autopsy?
Maybe the question answers itself with a "famous politician" involved. Dr. Mills does not strike one as a person who spends his time looking for trouble. Actually, Dr. Mills has given several reasons here, none of which are really sound. The most charitable thing to say is that the failure to perform an autopsy was the result of incompetency at a high level.

24. Why did Chief Arena never ask the Senator the reason for the nine hour delay in reporting the accident?
If you forget, right or wrong, there is nothing at all unusual in a small town official walking softly around a United States senator. Self-preservation is the first law of nature.

25. Why did Chief Arena dispose of the Senator's original confession statement and hand over the Keough purse for return to its owner before the inquest?
The chief was satisfied with the signed "original" he copied from the handwritten statement drawn up by Markham which the chief later indicated was thrown away—no showing or claim of harm has been made here, only an irregularity. The chief had no intention of investigating the case so he gave the purse back to Keough (which was found in the submerged car).

26. Why was District Attorney Dinis so reluctant to prosecute?
Politics reared its ugly head. In addition, this was a "hot potato" that, at first, looked as though it could be avoided. Dinis was no dummy.

27. Why did the Senator first say he got into a car at the cottage and asked to be taken to Edgartown, instead of telling of his return to the accident scene and of swimming back to Edgartown?
The question presupposes "truth" in some of the claims made by the Senator, and "truth" has been a very elusive quality in

this case. Whether any or all parts of the question are true, it is important only as it affects credibility—and the credibility of the Senator has yet to be established in any particular incident in the case.

28. Why did the Senator say he immediately contacted the police the next morning as soon as he fully realized what had happened? Why didn't he fully realize this after Markham and Gargan had unsuccessfully searched the pond?
This assumes the truth of the rescue operations under the auspices of Messrs. Markham and Gargan—we don't believe it. The Senator's use of "full realization" has not satisfied many people, including his own friends; particularly as 17 or more phone calls were made by or on behalf of the Senator before the "full realization" became fully activated. The Senator does not concede his audience's intelligence in this approach.

29. Why in his TV speech, did the Senator not explain the contradictions between that speech and the statement given to the police after the accident? Why did he omit his Saturday morning half-hour chat with Richards before he reported the accident?
The TV speech was professionally written and designed to build up good will and sympathy for the Senator. The speech was never intended to explain contradictions or tell the facts of Chappaquiddick.

30. Why did the Senator insist on a secret inquest?
The Senator claimed that his lawyers insisted on a closed inquest against his wishes, that he wanted everything made public but was overruled by his lawyers—this isn't even a good lie. They wanted the secrecy for the same general reason they have suppressed the facts whenever possible: WHAT THE PUBLIC DOESN'T KNOW CAN'T HURT THE SENATOR.

31. At the inquest Tretter said Gargan had told the girls that he and Markham had dived in after the Senator when he started his swim

across the channel to Edgartown. Why didn't Gargan or Markham testify to that at the inquest?
Because it would have been perjury. When (or if) Gargan made such a statement to the girls he was not under oath and, possibly, they were still fumbling around about what story they would tell.

32.   There are contradictions in the girls' testimony on how Markham and Gargan looked and acted when they returned to the cottage about 2:30 a.m. Why wasn't this pursued?
Judge Boyle ran the show with a tight and far too restrictive rein that prevented the pursuit of almost anything. Also, Mr. Dinis, who appeared on behalf of the people, had lost all interest in the matter long before the inquest. Basically, the inquest turned out to be a *pro forma* performance with everyone going through the motions in order to get rid of the matter.

33.   Since Judge Boyle had the authority, why did he not order the Senator's arrest and trial after finding "probable cause" (in the inquest) that the Senator's negligence had contributed to Mary Jo's death?
Judge Boyle did not even recommend that the Senator be prosecuted, let alone order his arrest and trial. The why is something only the judge can answer, and he retired after the inquest. One can conclude that truth and justice were never the objects of any of the Chappaquiddick legal procedures.

34.   Why was the grand jury refused the use of the inquest transcript in investigating Mary Jo's death?
Ask Judge Wilfred J. Pacquet of the Kennedy barony about this — he is the court jester who threw this and other curves that struck out the grand jury.

35.   It is claimed that District Attorney Dinis tried to discourage the grand jury. Since he knew the inquest facts, why did he request a grand jury? Was his coming re-election on the Kennedy ticket coincidental?
Dinis did not request the grand jury. He didn't ask for it, he didn't want it, and neither did the Massachusetts courts. The

grand jury "investigation" was brought about singlehandedly by Leslie Leland, the foreman who was tired of having his state and community placed in a bad light by the Chappaquiddick affair. It didn't do any good. Dinis did try to discourage the grand jury, and he knew he would be running on the same ticket with Kennedy in the fall of 1970—which was coincidental, but never left Dinis' mind.

36.   After the grand jury adjourned, why did the Senator's attorneys ask that the inquest proceedings be made public?
It was strictly grandstanding to make their client look good. As soon as the grand jury announced "no true bills" to Judge Pacquet, this fulfilled one of the grounds for release of the proceedings as set out by the Massachusetts Supreme Court in its secrecy order of October 30, 1969 regarding the inquest. The release of the transcript became a matter of mere routine.

37.   Why did the Massachusetts Supreme Court order release of the transcript after the grand jury had adjourned?
Basically the same answer. On its face, it would be because neither the grand jury nor the people ever had a chance.

38.   Do all of the Kennedy parties resemble a temperance picnic?
No. Do any of them? No.

39.   What was the significance of Mary Jo's blood alcohol content?
It meant, despite all of the sworn testimony to the contrary, that she had 4 or 5 ounces of hard liquor within the last hour alone before her death. It would mean a more substantial amount if she had been drinking more than an hour before her death, as alcohol disappears from the system unless replenished. The party had lasted several hours, and Senator Kennedy poured Mary Jo's first drink at about 8:30 p.m.

40.   What was the significance of the blood stains on Mary Jo's blouse?
They were not blood, there were no cuts, scratches, wounds or breaks on the body. The "stains" were from grass or other growing greenery which react to benzidine as blood. The

stains were on the back of the blouse, backs of the sleeves and back of the collar—no place else. This indicates the stains came from lying or leaning back onto grass or other greenery—which helps account for the "lost hour" between 11:15 p.m. and 12:45 a.m.

41. Why did Chief Arena whitewash Kennedy in court?
Throughout the case, the Chief was obviously awed by Edward M. Kennedy, United States Senator, and helped him in every way possible. Face it—the name Kennedy is the most powerful in Massachusetts.

42. Why no autopsy?
Dr. Mills, who examined the body, was guilty of all kinds of vacillation, and this gave the Kennedys—who never vacillate—the chance to get the body off the island and out of the jurisdiction of Massachusetts. The Senator made telephone arrangements for this before he reported the accident to Chief Arena.

43. Will the truth about Chappaquiddick ever be known?
Substantially speaking, the truth is known now. Senator Kennedy, due to intoxication and/or negligence, ran his car off the bridge; because of the manner in which the car hit and sank, the Senator was able to get out but Mary Jo was not. Since then, he has repeatedly falsified the facts of the case to help his political future.

Acknowledgments

and

Bibliography

ACKNOWLEDGMENTS AND BIBLIOGRAPHY

Our appreciation goes out to:

Human Events for the use of their files and material.

Jack Anderson and his Washington Merry-Go-Round column, and the kindness of his staff, including Miss Monk, for assisting our research.

The Republican National Committee and their Librarian, Miss Blondell, for the use of their files and library.

The Washington Post and Editor Ben Bradlee for the use of the Post Library which is the only place on the East Coast outside of the Edgartown Court House where the transcript of the inquest record could be found.

The personnel of: the Atlanta Public Library, the McAllen (Texas) Memorial Library, the San Antonio Public Library, the Library of Congress in Washington, D.C., the Bar Association Library at Edinburg, Hidalgo County, Texas, and Southmost College Library at Brownsville, Texas.

Other source material:

Burton Hersh, *The Education of Edward Kennedy*. New York: Morrow, 1972.

Zad Rust, *Teddy Bare*. Belmont, Mass.: Western Islands, 1971.

Jack Olsen, *The Bridge at Chappaquiddick*. Boston: Little, Brown, 1970.

Lester David, *Ted Kennedy: Triumphs and Tragedies.* New York: Grosset and Dunlap, 1972.

William H. Honan, *Ted Kennedy: Profile of a Survivor.* New York: Manor Books, 1972.

Robert Sherrill, "Chappaquiddick + 5." *The New York Times Magazine,* July 14, 1974.

Time magazine, various issues.

Newspapers, magazines and press association reports.

Extensive personal investigation and study.

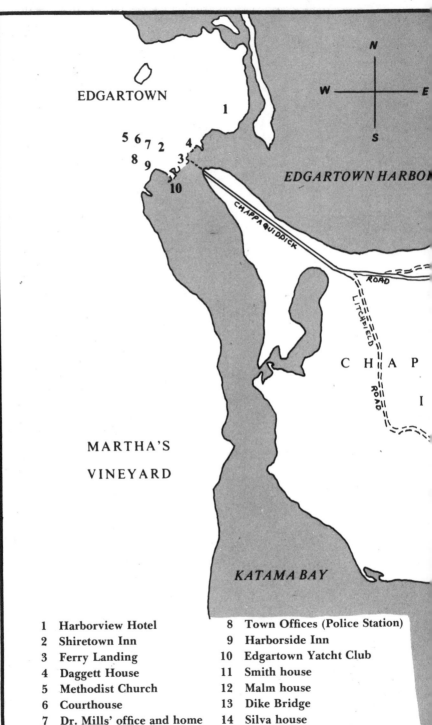

EDGARTOWN

N
W — E
S

1

5 6 7 2 4
8 9 3
10

EDGARTOWN HARBOR

CHAPPAQUIDDICK

ROAD

LITCHFIELD ROAD

C H A P

I

MARTHA'S
VINEYARD

KATAMA BAY

1 Harborview Hotel
2 Shiretown Inn
3 Ferry Landing
4 Daggett House
5 Methodist Church
6 Courthouse
7 Dr. Mills' office and home

8 Town Offices (Police Station)
9 Harborside Inn
10 Edgartown Yatcht Club
11 Smith house
12 Malm house
13 Dike Bridge
14 Silva house
15 Lawrence cottage